Man ... Quali...   ....red on or before
Higher E...ca...on

SRHE and Open University Press Imprint
General Editor: Heather Eggins

Current titles include:

Catherine Bargh *et al.*: *Governing Universities*
Catherine Bargh *et al.*: *University Leadership*
Ronald Barnett: *The Idea of Higher Education*
Ronald Barnett: *The Limits of Competence*
Ronald Barnett: *Higher Education*
Ronald Barnett: *Realizing the University in an age of supercomplexity*
Neville Bennett *et al.*: *Skills Development in Higher Education and Employment*
John Biggs: *Teaching for Quality Learning at University*
David Boud *et al.* (eds): *Using Experience for Learning*
Etienne Bourgeois *et al.*: *The Adult University*
Tom Bourner *et al.* (eds): *New Directions in Professional Higher Education*
John Brennan and Tarla Shah: *Managing Quality in Higher Education*
John Brennan *et al.* (eds): *What Kind of University?*
Anne Brockbank and Ian McGill: *Facilitating Reflective Learning in Higher Education*
Stephen Brookfield and Stephen Preskill: *Discussion as a Way of Teaching*
Sally Brown and Angela Glasner (eds): *Assessment Matters in Higher Education*
John Cowan: *On Becoming an Innovative University Teacher*
Heather Eggins (ed.): *Women as Leaders and Managers in Higher Education*
Gillian Evans: *Calling Academia to Account*
David Farnham (ed.): *Managing Academic Staff in Changing University Systems*
Sinclair Goodlad: *The Quest for Quality*
Harry Gray (ed.): *Universities and the Creation of Wealth*
Norman Jackson and Helen Lund (eds): *Benchmarking for Higher Education*
Merle Jacob and Tomas Hellström (eds): *The Future of Knowledge Production in the Academy*
Mary Lea and Barry Stierer (eds): *Student Writing in Higher Education*
Elaine Martin: *Changing Academic Work*
David Palfreyman and David Warner (eds): *Higher Education and the Law*
Craig Prichard: *Making Managers in Universities and Colleges*
Michael Prosser and Keith Trigwell: *Understanding Learning and Teaching*
John T. E. Richardson: *Researching Student Learning*
Stephen Rowland: *The Enquiring University Teacher*
Yoni Ryan and Ortrun Zuber-Skerritt (eds): *Supervising Postgraduates from Non-English Speaking Backgrounds*
Maggi Savin-Baden: *Problem-based Learning in Higher Education*
Peter Scott (ed.): *The Globalization of Higher Education*
Peter Scott: *The Meanings of Mass Higher Education*
Anthony Smith and Frank Webster (eds): *The Postmodern University?*
Imogen Taylor: *Developing Learning in Professional Education*
Peter G. Taylor: *Making Sense of Academic Life*
Susan Toohey: *Designing Courses for Higher Education*
Paul R. Trowler: *Academics Responding to Change*
David Warner and Elaine Crosthwaite (eds): *Human Resource Management in Higher and Further Education*
David Warner and Charles Leonard: *The Income Generation Handbook* (Second Edition)
David Warner and David Palfreyman (eds): *Higher Education Management*
Diana Woodward and Karen Ross: *Managing Equal Opportunities in Higher Education*

Managing Quality in Higher Education

An International Perspective on Institutional Assessment and Change

John Brennan and Tarla Shah

Organisation for Economic Co-operation and Development
The Society for Research into Higher Education
& Open University Press

Published by OECD, SRHE and
Open University Press
Celtic Court
22 Ballmoor
Buckingham
MK18 1XW

email: enquiries@openup.co.uk
world wide web: www.openup.co.uk

and
325 Chestnut Street
Philadelphia, PA 19106, USA

First Published 2000

ISBN   0 335 20673 5 (pb)   0 335 20674 3 (hb)

A catalogue record of this book is available from the British Library

Library of Congress Cataloging-in-Publication Data
Brennan, J. L. (John Leslie), 1947–
    Managing quality in higher education : an international perspective on institutional assessment and change/John Brennan and Tarla Shah.
        p.   cm.
    Includes bibliographical references and index.
    ISBN 0-335-20674-3 (hard) – ISBN 0-335-20673-5 (pbk.)
    1. Education, Higher–Evaluation–Case studies. 2. Total quality management–Case studies. I. Shah, Tarla, 1960– II. Title.
LB2331.62.B74 2000
378.1'01–dc21   99-088069

Copy-edited and typeset by The Running Head Limited, www.therunninghead.com
Printed in Great Britain by St Edmundsbury Press, Bury St Edmunds, Suffolk

Contents

Preface

This book is the outcome of a project sponsored by the OECD Programme on Institutional Management in Higher Education (IMHE), with support from the European Commission and the Higher Education Funding Council for England. The project was entitled 'Quality Management, Quality Assessment and the Decision-Making Process' and had two main objectives: (1) to clarify the purposes, methods and intended outcomes of different national systems of quality assessment, and (2) to investigate their impact on institutional management and decision-making. The latter was achieved through a series of institutional and national quality agency case studies.

First and foremost, therefore, we would like to thank all the authors of both the institutional and national quality agency case studies without whose contribution this book could not have been written. We would also like to thank Pierre Laderrière, firstly as the source of much stimulation and assistance during the course of the project in his capacity as Head of the IMHE Programme, and then for his contribution as 'critical reader' of an early draft of the book. Our thanks also to Tony Becher, another critical reader, for his useful comments and suggestions on the overall structure and contents of the book. We are very grateful to Jacqueline Smith of IMHE for her assistance in the co-ordination, liaison with authors and publication of the case studies. We would also like to acknowledge the contribution of Vin Massaro, Palle Rasmussen and the late Paul LeVasseur to the project design, in particular the nature and scope of the case studies. Finally, our thanks to Deana Parker for her invaluable assistance during the preparation of the book.

1

Introduction

The assessment and management of quality in higher education seems to arouse enthusiasm and cynicism in roughly equal measure. The enthusiasts proclaim an array of benefits to higher education institutions and the people who work and study in them. The cynics see, at best, futility and, at worst, serious damage to the academic enterprise. Neither group, we would suggest, has a lot of evidence on which to base their views.

New national arrangements for the assessment of quality have been introduced into higher education systems in many parts of the world only recently. They are part of radical changes which are occurring within institutions of higher education and in the relationships between the institutions and their host societies. Quality assessment is of particular interest in attempting to understand these changes because, as we shall see, it concerns both the traditionally private 'inner worlds' of higher education institutions and the political and social contexts which are increasingly important in shaping these worlds. Quality assessment links the private micro world of the institution with the public macro world of society and politics.

The growth of quality assessment can be likened to the growth of a world religion, a religion whose believers are divided into many different sects and who confront non-believers daily in their working lives. The sects tend to be evangelical, seeking to spread their views of the world to others and, like other religions, frequently enter into uneasy alliances with secular powers (the king, the rector, the government) to achieve their ends. In many cases it may be suspected that it is the secular power which is using the religion to pursue *its* ends.[1] Religious zeal of course generates scepticism among non-believers. It is not a good basis for dispassionate analysis. It is likely to be a source of conflict between different faiths and between the faithful and people who have none. The authors of this book are agnostic about the benefits and threats of quality assessment. Our approach is that it 'all depends': on how it is undertaken, in what context and for what purpose. Not very thrilling conclusions, it might be thought, but conclusions which we believe are warranted by the weight of the evidence available about the operation of quality assessment processes in higher education.

The rise of quality assessment has been stimulated by forces mainly from outside higher education institutions. These include the direct actions of governments in establishing national agencies for the assessment of quality in higher education. They include the pressures on institutions caused by expansion, diversification and cuts in funding levels. They include the importation of management cultures from business and manufacturing industry into the public sector generally, and education in particular. These forces have been contested to a greater or lesser extent within higher education. Organizational cultures which have traditionally involved high levels of personal autonomy and individualism do not embrace enthusiastically imposed policies which seem to have strong elements of conformity and regulation and whose stated purposes may frequently seem obscure and unwelcome. And yet many of the processes which underlie quality assessment provide opportunities for change and improvement in institutions. They can provide new sources of motivation and recognition for staff. They can provide greater institutional self-knowledge, as a resource for better decision-making within the institution and as a source of information to inform the choices and decisions of external users.

'Quality' in higher education was not invented in the 1990s. Universities and other institutions of higher education have always possessed mechanisms for assuring the quality of their work. Many of these concerned the quality of people: the qualifications necessary for students to gain admission and subsequently to gain a degree; the qualifications necessary to be appointed to an academic post or to achieve promotion to professor. Evaluation through peer review of research and publications was and is a further important element of traditional 'people' approaches to quality in higher education.

If 'find good people and let them get on with it' characterizes these traditional approaches to quality in higher education, they are frequently complemented today by processes which regulate *how* people 'get on with it', which require them to continuously *demonstrate* satisfactory 'performance', which encourage them to *improve*, which provide new systems of *rewards* and *sanctions*, which involve shifts in the locus of *authority* within higher education institutions and between those institutions and the state and other parts of society.

These processes of quality assessment as experienced by higher education institutions in 14 countries are the focus of this book. Our purpose is not to show how quality assessment should be done, but to consider the consequences of doing it at all, and the different consequences of doing it in different ways. As far as possible, we have attempted to be neutral about the processes which we describe and seek to analyse. This is not a book of advocacy, still less a book of prescriptions. Although we hope that many readers will find things of practical value in the chapters which follow, our greater concern is to attempt to inform and illuminate, and indeed to stimulate debate and appraisal of major changes which are taking place in higher education and in which, we would argue, quality assessment is playing a significant part.

The book is based on a project supported by the Programme on Institutional Management in Higher Education (IMHE) of the Organisation for Economic Co-operation and Development (OECD) and entitled 'Quality Management,

Quality Assessment and the Decision-Making Process'.[2] The project had two objectives: (1) to clarify the purposes, methods and intended outcomes of different national systems of quality assessment, and (2) to investigate their impact on institutional management and decision-making. The latter was achieved through a series of institutional case studies, undertaken by the institutions themselves but following a common framework. The institutional case studies were augmented by reports prepared by several national quality agencies on the agencies' own perceptions of their effects on their respective higher education communities,[3] as well as by relevant research literature.

A consideration of the adequacy of the case study method to the objectives of the project is necessary. The framework for the institutional case studies comprised the following elements: contexts, internal quality assurance methods, impact upon management and decision-making, other kinds of impact, departmental case studies, interpretation of outcomes of quality assessment and how these were related to the institution's mission and future strategies. A related framework for the national agency reports comprised contexts, audiences for quality assessment, internal quality assurance methods, effects on management and decision-making, other effects, system-wide outcomes, political and social support. Both frameworks emphasized the importance of considering all of the suggested elements in the context of institutional and system change. The framework documents provided additional guidance about issues to be addressed. The framework for the institutional case studies also contained a suggested 'framework for analysis' based on the approach taken in one of the early case studies, one of three pilots (Rasmussen, 1997).

A number of other features of the case studies need to be borne in mind. First, the participating institutions were self-selecting. The member institutions of the OECD Programme on Institutional Management in Higher Education were invited to participate in the project and 35 institutions from 16 countries responded positively to the invitation. Their willingness to take part in the project would suggest that these institutions had interests in quality issues at a fairly senior institutional level (the point of contact for the project) and, perhaps, that they felt that they had a good story to tell. In the event, 29 institutions and seven national quality agencies from 17 countries actually completed case studies.

Second, the authors of the case studies were staff members of the institutions. This brought with it both the advantages and disadvantages of familiarity and involvement with the inner lives of the institutions. A majority of the authors were senior administrators within their institutions and might be expected to provide an 'official' view of the situation, or at any rate a perspective reflecting their position and interests within the institution. Other case studies were written by social scientists based in particular departments, providing a different perspective on events.

Third, the authors and their institutions received no payment for their participation in the project. This is a relevant point because it implied a motivation based on enthusiasm and commitment rather than contractual relationships. However, it also entailed some limitations. Work on the project had to be fitted in around normal duties. This meant that the case studies varied considerably in terms of length and detail and the extent to which they were based on institutional research and analysis. It also meant that the timetable for the case studies inevitably slipped substantially. As they were undertaken on a purely voluntary basis, the project director was in no position to insist on details of content, method and timetable.

For all of these reasons, the information base for the project, although extensive, should not be regarded as necessarily representative of developments in quality assessment in the 17 participating countries. The features of institutional commitment, administrator perspectives, self-selection and self-study need continuously to be borne in mind in interpreting the data contained in the case studies. That said, a reading of the case studies will reveal the very high quality which many of the studies achieved. Authors were admirably self-critical, analytic and honest about the problems that their institutions were facing and the ways in which quality processes were being used to try to resolve them. In almost all cases, the perspectives of the case-study authors were supported by evidence. That they did not tell the whole story is hardly surprising. Perspectives drawn more substantially from other key institutional players – for example, teaching staff and researchers – would be partial in a different way.[4]

In considering the limitations of the data at our disposal, we count ourselves fortunate that we had credible data at all. Much of the literature on quality in higher education appears to lack any significant empirical base. Consequently, outcomes are assumed to be the intended ones, policies are equated with practices, advocacy is frequently a substitute for analysis. The data on which this book is based are substantial but, like any data, require interpretation. The above points are intended to help that interpretation. Where appropriate, we have drawn on other studies where these provide complementary perspectives to those of the case studies undertaken for the project. Details of the case-study sample and framework are contained in the appendices.

There is an additional methodological point to be made which applies to both aspects of the project, i.e. the analysis of national systems as well as the institutional case studies. As already noted, the former aspect of the project was undertaken through a mixture of literature review and consultation with national quality agencies. However, during the course of the project, several agencies altered their policies and methods, some new agencies were created and one or two ceased to operate. National policies on quality in higher education appear to be quite unstable in many countries. Many changes took place during the course of the project. Therefore, it should not be assumed that the policies and practices described in later chapters are necessarily the current ones in every detail in the countries concerned. We do not see this as a limitation to the project. Our objectives are primarily conceptual and analytic, and yesterday's practices are of as much interest as today's (or tomorrow's).

The same point about the rapidity of policy and procedural change applies equally to the higher education institutions. Not only are the external pressures and requirements on them changing, but institutions are learning and adapting in the light of experience. Therefore, in some cases institutional life will have moved on since the case studies were written. In particular, and this is a point to which we will return later, there is a difference between the initial impact of the introduction of quality assessment in an institution and the subsequent effects of quality assessment when processes have become more familiar and regularized. Again, for purposes of conceptualization and analysis, these features do not present problems.

It is partly for the above reasons that the issue of institutional change figures so strongly in this book and in its title. Changes in approaches to quality in higher education are intimately bound up with much wider changes being experienced by higher education, both internally and in its relations to society. The extent to which quality assessment is actually driving changes or is rather a product of them is a complex question which we shall address in later chapters.

So far we have used quality assessment as a generic term to describe the processes which are the concern of this book. A large and potentially bewildering terminology has built up around the quality movement in higher education. There is a lack of consistency and precision in the use of terms which becomes exacerbated when cross-national analysis is attempted. Although specialist definitions are available from a variety of sources (e.g. Harvey and Green, 1993; Frazer, 1997), terminology tends to be used loosely and interchangeably within higher education institutions. This vagueness of terminology is of interest in its own right: it enables people to read their own meanings into quality processes; it is a cause of their intellectual critique by academic staff (although it has to be allowed that disciplinary cultures differ substantially in their tolerance of ambiguity); and it is a cause of misunderstanding and sometimes of suspicion.

It is not our intention to attempt to create new – or endorse existing – terminologies of quality. But there is one important distinction which does need to be kept in mind, namely that between processes which are concerned with the judgement or measurement of quality and the decisions and actions which might need to be taken as a result of those judgements and measurements. We will generally use 'quality assessment' to describe the first more limited set of processes – evaluation, review, audit, monitoring are among the other terms which are commonly used. We will use 'quality management' as a more general term to describe the total process of judgement, decision and action. Quality assurance and quality control are other terms commonly used: control generally implies a regulatory function whereas assurance and management can involve both regulation and development or enhancement. In opting for the term quality management, we are not adopting or advocating a 'managerial approach' to quality, still less are we necessarily endorsing particular management ideologies such as Total Quality Management. We are using quality management as a generic term to cover all structures and processes, internal as well as external, involved in assuring quality in higher education. Arrangements for the *assessment* of quality form an important part of quality management. Most of this book concerns quality assessment – its rationale, its methods, its consequences – but broader processes of quality management are important background factors in most higher education institutions.

There is one other term that should be mentioned. Accreditation has been an important feature of quality management in North America for more than a century and has been adopted in other places more recently, for example in the new democracies of central and eastern Europe (EC PHARE, 1998a). The term is sometimes used as a general one to describe all aspects of quality management. To avoid confusion with other terms and processes, we shall use accreditation to refer to an achieved status awarded to an institution or programme by an authorized body. The accreditation decision is frequently based on the results of an assessment or evaluation process, but it need not be. Similarly, assessment or evaluation can be undertaken with no link to accreditation, and sometimes with no direct link to formal decision-making of any kind.

The experiences of the 29 higher education institutions and seven national quality agencies which took part in the project provide a large and complex repository of information about the interplay between developments in quality management and the many other changes which are taking place in higher education institutions. It is not straightforward to attempt to make broad generalizations from very disparate experiences. In order to do so, we have adopted a simple conceptual model of the impact of quality management and assessment which sees it as a function of the national and institutional contexts combined with the quality assessment methods used. The elements of the model are described in Chapter 2, which also includes discussions of the values and politics of quality assessment. The rest of the book is organized around the main elements of the model.

Chapters 3 and 4 deal with contexts. Chapter 3 considers the changing national contexts which have given rise to growing concerns about quality in higher education and the emergence of national systems for its assessment. These contexts include: the expansion of higher education, incorporating the growth of existing institutions as well as the creation of new ones; the diversification of higher education, in terms of types of institutions, types of programmes, and types of students; changes to funding methods and formulae, usually involving cuts in the unit of resource. But above all, the contexts for quality management and assessment in most countries include changing relationships between higher education and the state, involving different conceptions and degrees of autonomy, but coupled with a greater emphasis on and new forms of public accountability. Chapter 3 continues with a consideration of the emergence during the 1990s of national agencies for the assessment of higher education quality, and discusses the different types of agency and their relationship to decision-making at both national and institutional levels.

Chapter 4 looks at changes in institutional contexts, in particular at changing notions of autonomy and accountability. Common experiences are of expansion, diversification and new types of students, of organizational change and a growth of managerialism. New requirements of external accountability impose a need for institutions to comply. Other demands arising from the external environment impose a need to change – organizationally, structurally and culturally. Important differences between institutional contexts which have a bearing on quality management and assessment include size, internal structure – especially the extent of devolved decision-making – status, leadership, the extent and nature of recent changes and whether these were internally generated or externally imposed. Consideration of national and institutional contexts must embrace tradition and history as well as contemporary issues.

Chapters 5 and 6 look at methods of quality assessment. Chapter 5 deals with the methods used by various national quality agencies. While a general model comprising a national agency, institutional self-evaluation, external peer review and published reports continues to have validity, it masks a whole range of differences in the methods used (van Vught and Westerheijden, 1993). These include the level of the assessment (institutional or programme); the focus of assessment (on teaching, research, administrative processes); the types of peers used (including how they are selected, and whether and how they are trained); the balance between the use of observation, interview or performance indicators; whether methods are standardized or variable to take into account different institutional types and characteristics; the nature of reports and other outcomes; and the links with decision-making, for example on accreditation or funding. Similarities and differences in the stated purposes of national quality agencies are considered in the light of other variations. Recent national developments in quality assessment have tended to concentrate on the assessment of teaching or educational functions of higher education. Research is frequently assessed separately from teaching by different organizations and using different methods. The case studies tended to focus on the assessment of teaching programmes rather than on research and their emphasis is reflected in this book.

At the institutional level, Chapter 6 discusses the wide range of approaches to quality management described in the institutional case studies. Some of these are quite clearly a direct response to the requirements of external quality agencies; others are in response to quite specific institutional needs. But in many cases, internal and external considerations interact with each other to shape institutional approaches and experiences. Methods used include self-evaluation, student feedback, staff appraisal, various forms of review and monitoring. Some include external – frequently international – inputs, some involve use of performance indicators of various kinds. Chapter 6 also considers the roles in the quality management arrangements of committees, managers and administrators, academic staff at various levels, and students. It considers the differences between ad hoc assessment and review procedures – set up to resolve particular problems or issues – and more systematic and regular approaches – for example, departmental reviews on an agreed cycle.

Chapters 7, 8 and 9 look at the impacts of quality management and assessment activities. Three broad types of impact are distinguished: impact through rewards (Chapter 7), impact through changes in policies and structures (Chapter 8), and impact through changing cultures (Chapter 9). All three chapters also distinguish between levels of impact: on individuals, on programmes or basic units, on institutions, on the national system. These chapters also consider the effects of both external and internal quality management processes.

Chapter 7 concentrates on quality management through rewards, the most commonly mentioned being rewards of money, reputation and influence. The sources of reward are also varied, the main ones being institutional managements, academic peers inside and outside institutions, the state or its agencies, and markets. Chapter 7 discusses how impact through rewards varies according to contexts and methods of assessment.

Chapter 8 looks at changing policies and structures at both institutional and departmental levels. Organizational changes might involve departmental amalgamations or even closures, shifts in the locus of authority and processes of decision-making. Curriculum changes might involve content or structure or both. Some policy changes might refer to cross-institutional issues (for example, approaches to internationalization, initiatives on staff development and training. Other policy changes might be faculty specific, for example relating to collaboration between departments. Chapter 8 also considers how the impact of quality management through changing policies and structures varies according to contexts and methods.

Among the changing cultural factors discussed in Chapter 9 is the emphasis placed on the teaching function in institutions and the new approaches being adopted; concerns about skills; the balance between disciplinary and generic institutional conceptions of quality; changing relationships between staff, for example from individual to more collective working practices; changing productivity requirements and responses to them. As in the two preceding chapters, variations in impact are discussed in relation to context and method.

The final chapter on quality management and institutional change asks whether quality management makes a difference and, if so, of what sort. The possible answers to the question are considered from the viewpoints of national agencies, higher education institutions and academic staff. In asking the supplementary question of who and what is quality management for, we shall try to argue that quality management in higher education is as much about power, values and change as it is about quality. That is why it is frequently a source of controversy and conflict. That is why it matters.

Notes

1. We are indebted to Professor Ulrich Teichler for this analogy.
2. At various stages of the project, support was also provided by the European Commission and the Higher Education Funding Council for England.
3. The institutional case studies are available on the IMHE web-site (www.oecd.org/els/edu/imhe). Three of the early case studies and other articles based on the project were included in Brennan, de Vries and Williams (1997).
4. A useful perspective which complements the OECD study is to be found in an Anglo-Norwegian-Swedish study undertaken by Mary Henkel and colleagues. See, for example, Bauer and Henkel (1998).

2

Quality Assessment in Higher Education: A Conceptual Model

Introduction

In this chapter, we set out the main elements of a model which we use to structure the rest of this book. We see the impact of quality assessment as a function of two things: (1) the methods used, and (2) the national and institutional contexts for their use. We identify four different levels of impact within institutions and a number of different mechanisms through which impact occurs.

Underlying the operation of the model are issues of power and values. These reflect a growing openness of higher education institutions to the interests of external constituencies and a re-balancing of interests and authority within institutions in response to this more intrusive external context. From this perspective, quality management is embroiled in attempts to change values and to empower new interests. No wonder it is sometimes a source of controversy.

The normative nature of much of the literature on quality management and assessment plus the recency of the introduction of new approaches to quality assessment in many countries may account for the relative absence of a literature on its effects or impact. Although there is a growing literature on approaches to and methods of quality assessment at both institutional and national levels (Kells, 1988 and 1992; Vroeijenstijn, 1995), very little of it addresses the effects of quality assessment on other educational and organizational processes in higher education. The effects are presumed to be the intended ones. Only fairly recently have empirically-based studies begun to emerge which examine the impact of quality assessment upon higher education institutions in those countries which have relatively well-established systems (Frederiks *et al.*, 1994; Brennan, Frederiks and Shah, 1997; Bauer and Henkel, 1998).

The IMHE study complements and extends these national studies by providing analyses of the impacts of quality assessment in 29 different higher education institutions and seven national quality agencies in 17 different higher education systems. This book is based on those analyses.[1] The national reports and institutional case studies that were prepared as part of the IMHE study followed a common framework in order to permit comparability. Nevertheless, the

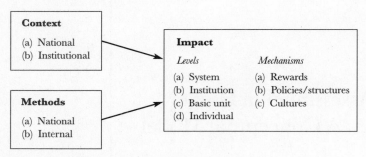

Figure 2.1   The impact of quality assessment

over-riding impression from reading them is one of variety and complexity, both in the way quality assessment has been carried out and in the national and institutional contexts in which it has occurred. The extent to which differences in method and context determine the impact of quality assessment is the major theme of this book. That quality assessment has an impact appears to us to be undeniable from a reading of the case studies. Whether the impacts are wholly desirable is a matter on which readers will draw their own conclusions. Whether the impacts are universal or dependent upon method and context will be the subject of the following chapters.

Figure 2.1 summarizes the relationships which are explored in the following chapters. The figure assumes that the nature of the impact of quality assessment differs between institutions and that these differences can be related to the methods used and to the institutional and national contexts for their use.

The contexts for quality assessment

The broader contextual changes which are affecting higher education have already been referred to in Chapter 1. Here we shall mention contextual factors which bear upon the impact of quality assessment and introduce some of the key variations in context which were highlighted by the IMHE case studies. In considering the contexts for quality assessment, it is necessary to distinguish between national and institutional factors.

At the national level, we find a set of factors which are common to most countries. Higher education systems have expanded, involving the creation of new institutions and the growth of existing ones. Higher education has become more diverse, both in terms of types of institutions, types of programmes and types of students who enter them. Higher education has become more international, involving greater student and staff mobility and creating pressures for harmonization of qualifications and internationalization of curricula. In many countries, higher education has been subject to cuts in public funding, frequently accompanied by changes to funding formulae and pressures on institutions to seek alternative sources of funding. In some countries there has been a growth in the number of private institutions of higher education. These changes are often accompanied by changes in the mechanisms by which governments seek to steer higher education, frequently involving more institutional autonomy, more competition and more accountability. Quality assessment has been introduced as part of these changes in many countries.

However, as well as broad developments which are common to a large majority of countries, there are also considerable contextual differences between countries, not least in their histories, traditions and cultures. The extent and methods of state steering of higher education are key factors. In most of continental Europe, matters to do with curricula, staff appointments and promotions, awards and qualifications have been decided, at least formally, by the state. Elsewhere, such matters have been decided within individual higher education institutions. The exercise of state controls tends to be associated with relative uniformity across higher education. Greater institutional decision-making permits greater heterogeneity. It has been suggested that the more governments move in the direction of self-regulation and steering at a distance, the more they will seek to promote the strengthening of managerial authority within institutions as well as improved systems of accountability (Goedegebuure *et al.*, 1993).

Several commentators have pointed to recent convergence in the regulation of higher education systems, with the state reducing its direct controls over higher education in order to support greater autonomy, flexibility and diversity at the institutional level (Neave and van Vught, 1991). As part of this trend towards deregulation, systems of quality assessment have been established to replace more direct controls by the state. The emergence of national quality agencies has been a key factor in the changing national context of higher education in many countries over recent years. The work of these agencies is the focus of later chapters. Suffice it to say here that there are interesting differences between them in terms of their governance, purposes and methods. These differences help shape the contexts in which individual higher education institutions approach and experience the assessment of quality.

As well as the particularities of national context, each higher education institution provides its own contextual features for quality assessment. Factors such as size, structures, prestige, resources, mission, history and leadership are the sources of major differences between institutions. These features of institutional context combine with those of the national context to help shape the impact of quality assessment within the individual institution.

The methods of quality assessment

At one level, quality assessment methods appear to be similar between countries. At first inspection, many national systems accord with what van Vught and Westerheijden have described as a 'general model' of quality assessment (van Vught and Westerheijden, 1993). The elements of the model are (1) a national co-ordinating body, (2) institutional self-evaluation, (3) external evaluation by academic peers and (4) published reports.

In countries where the first of these elements is found, the other three elements generally follow. However, as we shall see in later chapters, it should not be implied that countries without national quality bodies – or other elements of the model – have no means of assessing and assuring the quality of their higher education.

Methods of quality assessment in higher education differ on a number of dimensions. Differences are to be found in who assesses what, how, and how often. A basic distinction is between external and internal assessment. Where both features are present, a distinction lies in who has the 'last word'. Self-assessment is often a first stage in a process which leads to an external assessment. But there are also many examples of external assessment contributing to an internally led process. The 'who' question can be divided into a whole set of subsidiary questions: Who initiated the assessment? Who carried it out? Who is expected to act on its results?

The 'what' question is partly a matter of level: the whole institution, a faculty, a department, a programme, an individual staff member. It is also a matter of focus: teaching, research, administration. Each focus can be broken down further, for example teaching may include content, pedagogy or both; administration may focus on quality management or more general matters of institutional management and administration; research may focus on intrinsic academic quality and/or relevance and application.

The 'how' question can have many answers. Surveys of student opinion, of performance and progression data, of the views of employers are all common. Self-evaluations or internal reviews are now a feature in many institutions although, as we shall see later, their nature varies significantly. Peer review remains dominant in the assessment of research and is increasingly applied to the assessment of education. There are substantial differences in who is regarded as a peer for assessment purposes.

The 'how often' question in part divides between continuous quality assessment processes and those which occur intermittently, but on a regular cycle. Most institutions also undertake 'one-off' assessments for particular purposes, for example to decide whether to merge two departments, or how to respond to a cut in funding.

The above are all relatively formal and explicit forms of quality assessment. To them must be added the many informal and implicit forms of assessment which are part and parcel of academic life, for example the advice given by a senior professor to a younger colleague, the enthusiasm (or its absence) of students, the reputation of academic colleagues as measured by such things as invitations to conferences and reviews of their publications. The publicity given to quality assessment in recent years has been mainly concerned with the growth of formal explicit forms of assessment. But the existence of older informal methods should not be forgotten.

Finally, it is worth noting the existence of systematic, theory-based approaches to quality assessment of which the many variations of Total Quality Management (TQM) are the most frequently referred to. These seem rarely to have been adopted for the assessment of academic processes within higher education although the assumptions on which they are based may have fed into the assessment of administrative processes. TQM may have had more impact on management rhetoric than it has had on academic practice (Kells, 1992).[2]

These variations in the methods of quality assessment combine with differences in context to produce different kinds of impact on higher education.

The impact of quality assessment

Various ways of conceptualizing the impact of quality assessment can be found in the literature (e.g. Frederiks *et al.*, 1994; Rasmussen, 1997; Maassen and Westerheijden, 1998). In our study, we use a model which distinguishes between the *institutional level* and the *mechanism* of impact. Levels could be the individual, the basic unit (which might be a course, a department or a faculty), the institution, or the national system. Mechanisms could be through rewards and incentives (not necessarily financial), policies and structures (e.g. changed committee or curriculum structures) and cultures (e.g. academic values, priorities and relationships). These will be considered in later chapters which draw on the case studies.

In much of the literature on quality assessment, the question of impact is treated as one of the extent of presumed improvement or enhancement. We would argue that this is one of the ideological problems of the debates about quality in higher education. Firstly, there is a failure to distinguish between intention and outcome (by both national and institutional quality managers). Secondly, there is a failure to distinguish between organizational action and educational consequence (e.g. a committee may be set up to solve a problem, it may produce recommendations, they may be acted upon, but the actions may fail to solve the problem). Thirdly, the notion of 'improvement' is ideological, assuming values and criteria against which educational quality is to be judged. Quality assessment is sometimes a means of challenging and attempting to change existing educational values. What is 'improvement' from one point of view may be 'damage' from another point of view.

One of the objectives of the IMHE project was to explore the impact of quality assessment upon decision-making processes and this is the focus of the case studies on which this book draws. Improved academic standards and learning outcomes may or may not have occurred: the case studies and the broader research literature are relatively silent on this. The focus is on decision-making: how decisions are made, by whom, against what criteria. How quality assessment is organized and managed is, therefore, importantly a question of power and the introduction of systems of quality assessment frequently involve changing the balance of power between the institutional and system levels identified above.

The final sections of this chapter consider further the relationship between quality assessment and questions of values and power within higher education.

Type 1 'Academic'	Subject focus – knowledge and curricula Professorial authority Quality values vary across institution
Type 2 'Managerial'	Institutional focus – policies and procedures Managerial authority Quality values invariant across institution
Type 3 'Pedagogic'	People focus – skills and competencies Staff developers/educationalist influence Quality values invariant across institution
Type 4 'Employment focus'	Output focus – graduate standards/learning outcomes Employment/professional authority Quality values both variant and invariant across institution

Figure 2.2   Values of quality

Values and quality assessment

Quality assessment is sometimes controversial because it challenges existing academic values and conceptions about what constitutes high quality higher education. In this book, we identify four main types of 'quality values' underpinning different approaches to quality assessment (Figure 2.2).

Type 1 is based on traditional academic values. Its focus is upon the subject field and its criteria of quality stem from the characteristics of the subject. It is normally associated with strong professorial authority and control and on academic hierarchy based on quite rigid socialization and induction processes into the subject community. Conceptions of quality are based on subject affiliation and vary across the institution, which has limited scope to define and assess quality. In external assessment systems, the 'invisible college' of subject peers may by-pass the authority of the institution and speak directly to its members. Type 1 academic values remain the significant ones in quality assessment although they seem likely to be challenged increasingly in the future.

Type 2 values we term 'managerial'. These are associated with an institutional focus of assessment, with a concern about procedures and structures, with an assumption that quality can be produced by 'good management'. Quality characteristics are thus regarded as invariant across the whole institution. TQM provides an underlying ideological justification for this approach. Potentially it is an approach that can apply equally to all the functions and activities of a higher education institution, not just the academic. Indeed, there may be relatively little direct focus on academic matters in this approach.

Type 3 quality values we have described as 'pedagogic'. The focus here is on people, on their teaching skills and classroom practice. It is strongly associated with training and staff development. Like Type 2, quality characteristics are regarded as invariant across the institution. There is little emphasis on the *content* of education but a lot of emphasis on its *delivery*.

Type 4 values are employment-focused. Emphasis is placed on graduate output characteristics, on standards and learning outcomes. It is an approach which takes account of 'customer' requirements where the customers are frequently regarded as the employers of graduates. It tends to take into account both subject specific and core characteristics of high quality education. Thus, quality comprises some features which are invariant across the institution and some which vary according to subject.

In practice, conceptions of quality in particular countries and institutions can entail several types of values. But the balance between the types differs. Where new arrangements for quality assessment challenge existing values, they are more likely to be resisted. Whether resistance is likely to be successful will depend on questions of power.

The politics of quality assessment

Quality assessment is controversial because it affects the distribution of power within higher education. Ownership and control over quality assessment are often disputed because quality assessment affects the allocation of scarce resources – status as much as funding. It also has symbolic force, being seen as a challenge to academic autonomy whether at the individual, institutional or system level. National quality bodies have to strike some kind of balance between representation of the interests of institutional management, the academic profession more widely, non-academic interests and the agents of the state. The achieved balance may not have much effect on how the body carries out its job, but it will affect how various interest groups react to its work.

Achieving legitimacy for their processes and outcomes is one of the difficult challenges for quality bodies. They need the support of the academic community to provide the foot soldiers necessary for peer review and to achieve acquiescence within the institutions for decisions reached. Legitimacy must also be achieved with the agents of the state if the results of quality assessment are to achieve credibility for policy and decision-making purposes at the national level. Although many within higher education are suspicious of the latter function, failure of the quality body to exercise it may expose higher education to the danger of other, and possibly more damaging, forms of direct state intervention.

Quality assessment also affects the balance of power within higher education institutions. Quality assessment at the subject or programme level can affect the status and influence of departments: a 'successful' assessment enhancing them, an 'unsuccessful' assessment damaging them. Quality assessment at the institutional level, by emphasizing the responsibilities exercised at that level, tends to strengthen institutional management. Indeed, most forms of quality assessment strengthen institutional management, providing it with information on which to base decisions and an external 'threat' to justify the need to take those decisions. However, running counter to the managerial impetus of quality assessment is the extension of the authority of subject communities by the use of peer review. Quality judgements made by subject specialists outside of the institution can lessen the likelihood of institutional management being able to achieve ends which run counter to those judgements.

Quality assessment can also affect *how* decisions are made. Quality assessment processes in education are generally transparent, involving face-to-face dialogue between assessors and assessed, published reports which provide evidence and reasons for judgements reached. As such, they are likely to support greater rationality in decision-making, enhancing the use of evidence and promoting the equal treatment of different groups and individuals. However, depending on the power and influence of existing interest groups in institutions (or in higher education systems), the results of quality assessment may be discounted to a greater or lesser extent, particularly if they threaten the interests of those groups.

Dependent on context and interests, quality assessment can be used in attack or defence. In attack, it is a tool available to the state and to institutional managements with which to control, and perhaps to transform, higher education. In defence, it can be used by academic and subject groups to help protect the maintenance of their values and, where the results of assessment allow, to claim a status (and associated rewards) that might otherwise be unavailable.

Finally, quality assessment can affect the relative powers of 'producers' and 'consumers'. Students can be empowered through quality assessment by contributing their views and experiences to the assessment process and by using the public outcomes of the assessment process in decisions about what and where to study. Potentially, a greater availability through quality assessment of information about the inner workings of higher education institutions strengthens the influence which people outside can bring to bear on them. As we shall see, variations in context and method of quality assessment affect all of this – for it determines the winners and the losers, threatens or empowers, radicalizes or maintains the status quo.

Much of the literature on higher education emphasizes the autonomy of institutions and the basic units within them and, in particular, the autonomy and power of tenured academic staff (Clark, 1983; Becher and Kogan, 1992). Quality assessment threatens this. By emphasizing collectivity, transparency and accountability, quality assessment seems destined to alter the organizational role of departmental leaders and senior academics within institutions. Whatever the variations in method, the emphasis of quality assessment on procedures and on conclusions based on evidence is at odds with conceptions of quality based on the status of individuals. Those who have traditionally enjoyed the most status and power within higher education institutions may be the greatest losers from the introduction of quality assessment (Figure 2.3).

Drawing on the work of the sociologist, Max Weber, Finch has drawn a distinction between 'naked power' and 'legitimate authority' with regard to decision-making in higher education (Finch, 1997: 152–3). Organizations which have genuine power, in Weber's terms, possess 'the ability to pursue their aims despite the resistance of others' (Finch, 1997: 153). Most national quality agencies arguably have such power. In most cases it is derived from the state and is linked, at least in principle, to the exercise of state power through legislation and funding. Rather more arguably, the managements of higher education

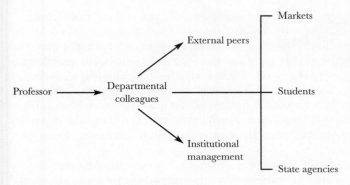

Figure 2.3   The loss of professorial power

institutions also possess 'naked power' although there remain considerable variations between institutions and countries in this respect. However, Weber believed that a stable society could not be based on the exercise of naked power: decisions made in this way would tend to be resisted or subverted. What was necessary was the conversion of naked power into legitimate authority. Legitimacy implies that people accept certain kinds of decisions as binding upon them. Legitimacy in higher education is commonly thought to be achieved through adherence to values and standards which are a part of the cultures of academic disciplines (Becher, 1989; Becher and Kogan, 1992; Finch, 1997).

Finch sets out the implications starkly:

> The whole of the academic enterprise depends on there being a reasonably clear collective understanding between academics in a given discipline that a particular piece of work counts as good and something else as less good. Without that collective understanding, academic disciplines really do not exist. Were that to disappear, the resulting intellectual anarchy would bring down the whole edifice, since there would be no reason at all why taxpayers should pay us to educate the young, nor why sponsors should pay us to conduct research.
>
> (Finch, 1997: 152)

Thus, for Finch, the role of peer review is central to the achievement of legitimacy for quality assessment processes and the decisions reached on the basis of them. We have made similar points in an earlier study of our own (Brennan *et al.*, 1994). Here we referred to the 'moral' authority of peers in contrast to the 'bureaucratic' authority of quality bodies. Finch believes that bureaucratic authority can only achieve legitimacy within higher education by co-opting the moral authority of academic peer groups. This is why virtually all quality bodies make peer review a central part of their assessment processes. Will this achieve legitimacy among academics? We argued in our previous study that this would not necessarily be so.

There are several reasons why peer group authority may be problematic in quality assessment. An obvious one is that the assessors might not be regarded as genuine peers by those on the receiving end. But even if their peer status is accepted, the assessors may be required to make their assessments not on the basis of the 'collective understanding' of the discipline but according to rules and guidelines issued by the quality body and reinforced through training and briefing. And where the focus of assessments lies outside of the boundaries of disciplinary competence, for example on institutional policies and procedures, it becomes difficult to define a peer in traditional disciplinary terms. Hence, legitimacy may become problematic. It is worth noting that several quality agencies do not refer to the notion of 'peer' in their methodology, preferring terms such as 'expert' or 'assessor'.

But does the academic legitimacy of quality assessment processes really matter? Does not quality assessment have to convince other more influential players – the state, potential students, employers of graduates, the sponsors of research? For these groups, legitimacy may be achieved through criteria other than disciplinary understandings – for example, customer satisfaction, value for money, relevance to economic growth.

Conclusion

In focusing attention on contentious matters such as values and power, we may be accused of seeing conflict where none exists, of neglecting the shared purposes of all those involved in quality management and assessment to ensure high quality and improvement in higher education. Yet we doubt whether such a consensual view is tenable within mass and diverse higher education systems.

The problem for quality assessment is that it must address several audiences and these different audiences may have different criteria for what constitutes quality and different reasons for wishing to assess it. Most quality bodies strive to achieve a composite conception of quality – perhaps including all of the values discussed in the previous section – that will achieve legitimacy with all relevant audiences. Where there is failure to achieve this, the words of another sociologist (Berger, 1966) might be paraphrased: 'He who has the biggest stick has the biggest chance of defining quality.' This sounds suspiciously like 'naked power' and its existence should not be forgotten in considering the effects of quality assessment.

Notes

1. The institutional case studies that were undertaken for the IMHE study are available on the IMHE Programme web page (www.oecd.org/els/edu/imhe).
2. Herb Kells has discussed critically the applicability of TQM approaches to higher education (Kells, 1992).

3

Changing National Contexts:
The Rise of Quality Management
Assessment

Introduction

The formal evaluation or assessment of higher education by national agencies is a contemporary phenomenon. Its appearance towards the end of the 1980s can be seen as part of broader trends towards new forms of accountability in the public services and the professions, a trend aptly characterized by Neave as the 'rise of the evaluative state' (Neave, 1988). It is also associated with the application of and confidence in 'management' as the key factor in determining the 'success' and 'productivity' of institutions of whatever sort. Although many writers have poured a certain amount of scorn on the claims of management theories and the associated vocabularies of the evaluative state (e.g. Salter and Tapper, 1994; Cowen, 1996; Kogan and Hanney, 1999), their critiques can often seem to harken back to previous 'romantic' ages of the university rather than to address the problems faced by the contemporary institution (Parker and Courtney, 1998).

The remark by Clark Kerr to the effect that, of the 85 institutions in the Western world which have existed from the sixteenth century to the present, 70 of them are universities, has been much quoted by writers on higher education:

> About eighty-five institutions in the Western world established by 1520 still exist in recognizable forms with similar functions and unbroken histories, including the Catholic Church, the parliaments of the Isle of Man, Iceland and Great Britain, several Swiss cantons, and seventy universities. Kings that rule, feudal lords with vassals, and guilds with monopolies are gone. These seventy universities, however, are still in the same locations with some of the same buildings, with professors and students doing much the same things, and with governance carried on in much the same way.
>
> (Kerr, 1982: 182)

No doubt the modern supermarket can also trace an ancestry to the medieval market place, although such a claim seems unlikely to afford any advantage for the former. Whatever the antiquity of the university idea and the survival of a small number of its organizational embodiments, most universities have been established in the second half of the twentieth century. (The average secondary school is almost certainly rather older than the average university.) The rise of evaluation and assessment in higher education has to be seen in the context of the characteristics of modern and vastly expanded higher education systems.

In this chapter we consider three features of the national contexts for higher education with which individual institutions must contend. The first of these is the size, structure and resourcing of the different national higher education systems. The second is the changing relationship between higher education and the state. The third rather more specific feature is the creation of national agencies for the assessment of higher education quality. The idea and application of the concept of accountability to higher education institutions will also be considered.

Expansion, diversification and funding cuts

A fivefold increase in student numbers over the last twenty years has been typical of the rate of increase in higher education enrolments in Western countries. Age participation rates have risen from under 10 per cent to over 30 per cent. Postgraduate student numbers have also risen dramatically. There are many more people working in universities and other higher education institutions, not only as researchers and teachers but also as administrators and support staff. Many new higher education institutions have been created and most existing ones have expanded substantially.

Expansion has raised costs and increased the visibility of higher education. Most students are first generation students. Through them, their parents and relatives and their future employers will learn something of higher education, will become interested parties in what goes on there. Their interests are likely to be what van Vught has described as 'extrinsic' interests, or 'the services higher education institutions provide to society' (van Vught, 1994: 32). Chief among these interests are whether students obtain jobs after their higher education and whether they are any good at doing them. Other interests will concern the costs involved, whether borne by the state or by individuals. Costs to the state – because of expansion – will be very much higher than in previous generations. Costs to the individual will be relatively higher and be more significant to the students and their families as larger numbers of students from lower income families enter higher education.

Expansion, by increasing costs and extending the numbers and types of people interested in higher education, draws attention to issues of quality. At the same time, it removes the prime traditional mechanisms for achieving it, namely exclusiveness. Small, elite systems of higher education could rest their claims to quality and excellence on selectivity: only the 'best' were admitted as students, only the most able were allowed to teach them. The fact that at many times in many places gaining entry to higher education had as much to do with social selectivity as with educational selectivity did not matter. There might well be 'more able' people outside the walls of higher education institutions, but they would not be recognized as such without the certificates bestowed by higher education. An elite could justify its social and economic advantages by reference to the qualities bestowed by a university education. The qualities of that university education could be demonstrated by reference to its exclusiveness.[1]

Expansion drew attention to issues of quality in higher education while removing the principal argument – exclusiveness – for demonstrating it. That many academics (and others) have so far failed to come to terms with the realities of expanded higher education systems is reflected in the continuing use in many countries of high entry qualifications as indicators of quality. It is worth remembering that the majority of people teaching and researching in today's mass higher education systems and institutions were themselves educated in smaller more elite ones. As Scott has suggested with regard to the British case, it is possible to create a mass system while retaining an elitist mentality for thinking about it (Scott, 1995).

With expansion has come diversity. Non-university sectors and institutions have been created in many countries through the upgrading and merging of existing colleges. Of the countries which took part in the IMHE study, only Australia and the United Kingdom had moved in the opposite direction by getting rid of most of their non-university institutions and creating mainly university systems. Even in these countries, however, non-university institutions continue to play a part in the development of mass higher education. Elsewhere, non-university sectors have long been important in France, Germany and the Netherlands and are of growing significance in Portugal, Norway and Finland.

Binary systems of higher education pose interesting questions of status allocation – which institutions may be called universities, which polytechnics and so on – and quality assessment processes are frequently involved in determining the answers. However, seen from a different perspective, binary systems of universities and non-university institutions may be viewed as representing very limited forms of diversity, maintaining rigid demarcations between two types of institution in contrast to a much richer variety of institutional forms and missions (Goedegebuure *et al.*, 1993; Scott, 1995). Such diversity has long existed in the United States – famously codified in the Carnegie classification of institutions – but is emerging more slowly, and with misgivings, in other parts of the world.

Diversity of institutions poses questions for public understanding. Diversity of function gets mixed up with hierarchy of status. Thus, British employers routinely prefer to recruit from the socially prestigious institutions even though the content of their curricula may be less relevant to the jobs they have on offer than the content of the courses at more lowly colleges, polytechnics or 'new' universities (Brennan *et al.*, 1993). Pierre Bourdieu has analysed extensively the role of French higher education institutions in the reproduction of its social elite

(Bourdieu, 1996). Similar analyses are available elsewhere (e.g. Adonis and Pollard, 1997; Whitty *et al.*, 1998). The confusion of social exclusivity with academic exclusivity in most higher education systems has major consequences for the esteem in which different kinds of institutions are held.

Functional diversity and status hierarchy increase with expansion but are not the same everywhere. German universities appear to enjoy a rough equivalence of esteem largely denied to their Anglo-Saxon (such as in the UK, North America, Australia and New Zealand) and French counterparts. Indeed, in the former group it could be argued that there is relatively little hierarchy or diversity. And Germany remains the one European country not to have established a national quality system, although a few of the individual Lander are developing arrangements along the lines of those operating in neighbouring countries, notably the Netherlands.[2]

Institutional diversity poses one set of potential confusions and concerns but, as Goedegebuure *et al.* (1993) point out, diversity in higher education is not limited to types of institution. Courses in new subject fields, courses geared towards new kinds of labour market need, and courses delivered by new forms of technology, leading in some cases to new types and levels of academic award, have produced an enormous growth in programme diversity. Diversity implies greater choice: not just of where to study but what to study and how. As we shall see, informing 'consumer' choice is frequently claimed to be an important function of quality assessment in higher education.

To diversity of institutions and programmes must be added increasing diversity of delivery. Open and distance learning, work-based learning, computer-assisted learning are but examples of the use of new technologies and forms of making higher education available. And these new forms pose questions for our traditional conceptions of higher education. Does good quality higher education require face-to-face contact between teacher and taught and interaction between students? How can the independence of student work be assured? What are the respective responsibilities and relations between the student, the employer and the university in work-based learning? Innovations in these and other ways raise issues of purposes and criteria of effectiveness. New forms of higher education face credibility problems which traditional forms do not. In higher education, it is *lack* of familiarity which can 'breed contempt', at least in some quarters.

Linked to diversity of institutions, programmes and delivery is a greater diversity of the student body. Students today enter higher education from a wider range of social and educational backgrounds, possess a wider range of expectations and motivations, and face a wider range of future destinations than did previous generations of students. In some countries, students are older – some of them much older – bringing with them a wide range of life experiences, quite possibly combining higher education with work and/or raising a family. These students in particular may lack traditional entry qualifications. Even if they have them, they may have obtained them some time ago. Lifelong learning brings with it the prospect of people returning to higher education several times. But learning needs in later life may differ greatly from initial higher education, and conceptions of educational levels may be challenged in the process. For at least some institutions, a greater diversity of the student body requires innovation and adaptation in teaching, learning and assessment methods as well as new kinds of support services concerned with counselling, work placement and careers advice.

Diversity implies choice: what kind of institution to be, what kind of programme to design, where and what to study, what sorts of graduates to hire, and what kinds of higher education to fund. Managers and academics, students and employers, the state and other funders all face choices which either did not exist or were much simpler only a generation ago.

One set of choices concerns funding, whether by the state or others: what to fund, at what level, and according to what formula. Expansion has made higher education more costly everywhere. And hardly anywhere have funding levels kept pace with expansion. Higher education may not always have been asked to do 'more with less' but it has been asked in recent years to do 'more with not enough' from the point of view of most higher education managers.

Many within higher education would of course argue that the single most important threat to maintaining quality is the deterioration in funding levels. Paradoxically, governments are laying great stress on quality at the same time as their actions on funding are doing most to jeopardize it. The extent to which processes of quality management get to grips with the relationship between funding and quality will be the subject of later chapters. But here should be noted the problems and challenges posed for higher education institutions from both the reduction in funding levels and the development of new funding allocation mechanisms. The extent and nature of these differ between countries – and frequently have different consequences for individual institutions within the same country – but universally the picture is one of change. The steady-state is not an option.

Expansion, diversification and cuts in funding levels are all aspects of change in higher education. Individual changes may be welcomed or resisted, depending upon viewpoints and interests. Change may be coped with by individual adaptation, collective action, 'scientific' management and planning; it may be confronted directly or ignored. Quality management is necessarily embroiled in both the consequences of changes in the past and the decisions to be made about those in the future. The next section looks at the management of change at the level of the higher education system.

Changing relations between higher education and the state

The process of change in higher education is often characterized by its incremental nature, driven largely by internal developments within individual disciplines. Change in higher education is seen as 'bottom-up' rather than as a result of policy direction or control at either institutional or system levels. As Cohen and March put it in a classic text:

Anything that requires a co-ordinated effort of the organization in order to start is unlikely to be started. Anything that requires a co-ordinated effort of the organization in order to be stopped is unlikely to be stopped.

(Cohen and March, 1974: 206)

It is certainly a characteristic of higher education institutions that their members have considerable capability to subvert the intentions of policies generated externally. But the scale and the nature of changes experienced by most institutions in recent years represent what Burton Clark has referred to as 'fundamental change' (Clark, 1983), i.e. structural change, change in authority over who does what under what conditions. The relationship between these fundamental changes and traditional forms of bottom-up incrementalism is far from clear. Many would argue that the essential characteristics of academic work are largely unchanged (though rendered more difficult) by broader higher education policies (Kogan and Hanney, 1999; Henkel, forthcoming). There are almost certainly major institutional differences in the impact of new policies and structures.

The relationship between higher education and its wider social environment is influenced increasingly in many countries by market conditions. Although the operation of markets in higher education is complex and their importance can be overstated, it is undeniable that higher education institutions increasingly find themselves competing for students, funding, staff and, above all, reputation. Additionally, governments frequently seek to increase the responsiveness of institutions through the appointment of business leaders and others from outside academe to serve on influential intermediary bodies and institutional governing boards.

In some countries, market conditions are replacing state controls as the principal mechanism of higher education steering. In many, relationships between higher education and the state are changing. In continental Europe, there is a general movement away from state authority. In the United States, however, some individual states are beginning to exert rather more authority. In Australia, the Federal Government appears to be becoming a more important player. From the point of view of the disciplinary base of the system, autonomy may be constrained by increasingly powerful institutional management, by state sponsored commissions or other intermediary bodies, by markets, or by direct legislation by the state (e.g. Becher and Kogan, 1992; Goedegebuure *et al.*, 1993).

It is not just forms of regulation which influence behaviour in educational institutions. Wider cultural factors will affect responses to change. Drawing on Hofstede's work on the culture of organizations (Hofstede, 1991), Kells has recently explored the impact of national cultural factors on the operation of quality assurance in higher education (Kells, 1998). He considers the effects of 'power distance' (the extent to which unequal power is regarded as socially justifiable), 'uncertainty avoidance' (intolerance of ambiguity), 'masculinity or femininity' and the balance between individualism and collectivism. While it may be rather difficult to assign individual countries to cultural types of this sort as Kells attempts, he is surely right to remind us of the importance of cultural factors, at institutional as well as national levels, in mediating the effects of apparently similar policies and procedures. However, it is equally important not to regard culture as static. Indeed, as we shall see in later chapters, changes in culture may be one of the effects of quality management and assessment as well as a factor which can mediate these effects.

Changes in culture and the exercise of authority can be related to the broader changes in higher education already discussed. In small 'elite' systems, access to higher education was restricted, socially and educationally, not just for students but for their teachers. The relative narrowness of entry supported a degree of value consensus among those within higher education which expansion has broken. Different goals and expectations compete for primacy both within and between institutions. Expanded systems have more extrinsic functions to perform, largely related to labour market needs. Accordingly, governments look for new mechanisms with which to steer higher education in desired directions. Imperatives derived from developments in research and scholarship within individual disciplines have to compete with considerations to do with making graduates more employable or with cutting costs.

There remain important differences between countries in how and where authority is exercised in higher education. The continental European model (whether in its Humboldtian or Napoleonic forms) has on the whole combined centralized state control with a powerful professoriate within institutions. Differences have existed and continue to exist in the extent and nature of state powers, the degree to which they are largely symbolic, the degree to which they are only exercised on the basis of influential academic advisory groups, and so on. What was common to these countries was the relative weakness of the higher education institutions and their leaderships. Real powers were roughly divided between state ministries and the professors within faculties and departments, with the two frequently by-passing the institution to do business directly with each other (see, e.g. Gellert, 1998).

The institutional level of decision-making was more important in other countries and continents. Anglo-Saxon traditions have generally been characterized by weak state control with greater power exercised at institutional levels. There have, though, been considerable differences in the powers of institutional managers and the powers of basic units (departments and faculties) with the latter tending to be exercised more democratically than in continental European systems. Elsewhere, for example in Latin America and South-East Asia, institutional levels of decision-making have been important, frequently set within market-driven rather than state-managed systems.

Considerable differences exist, therefore, between the traditions of decision-making in higher education in different countries, with the exercise of authority varying between the state, the institution, the basic academic unit, and the individual academic staff member. Decisions taken at all four levels determine higher education change. Decisions at different levels may be more or less responsive to the broader environmental changes sketched briefly above. Into these four levels of decision-making, and providing new forms of linkage between them, have come the activities of the new quality agencies. The agencies have posed new requirements for institutions and their basic units which have the potential to alter relationships between decision-makers at different levels and to affect the criteria on which decisions are made.

The emergence of national quality agencies

Although accreditation bodies have existed in the United States for most of the century, the emergence of quality agencies in Europe and elsewhere is a much more recent phenomenon. Indeed, in the course of the IMHE project, the numbers of quality agencies in western Europe have approximately doubled. In 1990, only France, the Netherlands and the United Kingdom possessed quality agencies. With the enthusiastic encouragement of the European Union (European Commission, 1995), virtually all countries have followed suit. And most countries in eastern Europe, where no such agencies existed at the time of the collapse of communism, have created them since, frequently with considerable expectations as to their capacity to both drive change and to regulate its consequences (EC PHARE, 1998a).

The relationship between the emergence of quality agencies and other changes occurring in higher education is complex. On the one hand, quality agencies appear to be drivers of change in higher education. On the other, they are changed to prevent unwanted consequences of changes occurring as the result of other factors. Several writers (e.g. Barnett, 1994; Vroeijenstijn, 1995) have referred to the accountability and improvement functions of quality assurance and the tensions which exist between them. There has been a tendency in the debates which have taken place in several countries to see improvement as 'good' and accountability as 'bad'. But, as already pointed out in the first chapter of this book, the normative nature of so much of the debate gets in the way of seeing exactly what is going on. By referring to concepts of authority and change, it is hoped that the emergence of quality agencies can be discussed in a more neutral way.

In countries where authority has been strong at the levels of the state and of individual professors, the management of change has faced particular difficulties. Decision-making at the state level is typically slow and cumbersome and is ill-equipped to deal with the increased diversity characteristic of modern higher education systems. Regulation by means of legal statute encourages conformity and protection of the status quo. This has been the tradition in continental Europe. It has tied the management of higher education to the exercise of state authority through a range of regulative mechanisms, for example staff employment and conditions of service, curriculum design and approval, funding and detailed financial control. At the same time, individual professors have been able to exercise considerable autonomy in their daily academic work and a dominant control over the activities of the units in which they are based. As already noted, relatively little authority was traditionally located at the institutional level in these countries. In consequence, decision-making at all levels has been ill-equipped to deal with the consequences of massification, diversity and funding cuts. State-level controls were insufficiently flexible, institutions lacked authority, and individual professors and basic units decided things in terms of individualistic and internal agendas.

In these circumstances, quality agencies could disturb the existing distribution of authority in a number of ways. First, they could help justify some relaxation of controls by the state. They could make it acceptable to transfer powers from the state to higher education institutions by providing a mechanism whereby the institutions would be accountable for the exercise of these newly acquired powers. The state might no longer be in direct *control* over what was going on in higher education, but at least it was in receipt of *knowledge* about it. Second, by transferring responsibilities to institutions, the managers of the institutions acquired more authority. Professors who had previously negotiated directly with ministries for their needs were now forced to deal with their rector. And third, review processes initiated by the agencies required *collective* responses at basic unit level which would necessitate some mediation of individualistic agendas. Thus, the conditions to support systematic change within higher education were enhanced with relatively limited sacrifice of state control.

Generalizations are difficult but, on the whole, state controls have traditionally been weaker outside of continental Europe.[3] Change has been less of a problem and existing institutions have diversified, new (sometimes private) institutions have been created and new markets and funding sources pursued through the establishment of new courses and other services. Burton Clark (1998) has described some of these 'entrepreneurial universities' and has attempted to identify their common elements. What is clear from Clark's study, and from the institutional case studies to be considered in Chapter 4, is that cuts in state funding for higher education have been major motivating forces for change and innovation in many places. But it is also the case that these funding cuts have also been perceived as posing threats to quality.

In systems characterized by low levels of state control, therefore, quality has become an issue because of the effects of funding cuts and the entrepreneurial responses of certain institutions to these cuts as well as the more general effects of expansion and diversity. In these circumstances, quality agencies have been perceived to have a more explicit control function (the generation of change was less of a problem than the control of its consequences). The agencies were perceived to challenge well-established traditions of institutional autonomy. Institutions were unused to external controls and therefore a 'quid pro quo' of relaxation of other controls (such as had existed in continental Europe) was not an option. Thus, the introduction of national quality agencies has tended to be more controversial outside of continental Europe (e.g. Australia, United Kingdom) almost irrespective of the methods and procedures used.

It is of course risky to make the sort of generalization summarized in Figure 3.1. National complicating factors exist in many countries, for example the antagonism of the Thatcher government to the universities, public services and the professions generally (Kogan and Kogan, 1984). It must also be admitted that the response of higher education to the introduction of quality assessment has differed according to the methods used. But traditions in the exercise of

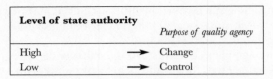

Level of state authority		
	Purpose of quality agency	
High	→	Change
Low	→	Control

Figure 3.1   State authority and the purpose of national quality agencies

authority and decision-making constitute important contextual factors which have influenced these responses.

National quality agencies exist within a more complex set of relationships between higher education and the state, of which funding is the most universal and generally most important. Where the state exercises direct control over funding, curriculum or licensing of higher education institutions, the results of national quality exercises can feed directly into decision-making on these matters. This is the case almost irrespective of the stated purposes and degree of independence of the agency. For example, the well-publicized Dutch quality assessment system has emphasized improvement as its major goal. It is owned collectively by the Dutch universities (Vroeijenstijn, 1994). Yet alongside this system exists an inspectorate of the Dutch ministry which oversees and enquires into the actions taken by universities in response to quality assessment. The inspectorate reports to the minister who has powers to close courses and even whole institutions. Such powers may be rarely used but their existence is an important element in the balance of power between higher education and the state. 'Reserve' powers of this sort have now also been introduced in Britain (held by the higher education funding councils rather than by the state directly) and may serve to reassure ministries on behalf of the public that adequate accountability exists. The licensing powers of individual states in the United States have been little remarked upon in comparison to the publicity accorded to accreditation, but their existence is an important context for the operation of accreditating procedures.

A supra-national element in Europe

Within western Europe during the 1990s, the national contextual factors which have given rise to the emergence of quality assessment have been complemented by European factors and by strongly worded recommendations from the European Union. Mobility of labour has resulted in emphasis being placed on the mutual recognition of qualifications between the member states. Increased collaboration across European higher education in terms of student and staff exchanges, joint curriculum initiatives and the like have entailed a need for greater transparency and understanding of systems and institutions.

In this context, the European Union issued a recommendation to its member states in 1997 to 'establish . . . transparent quality assessment and quality assurance systems' (European Commission, 1997). These were to have the following three aims:

- to safeguard the quality of higher education within the specific economic, social and cultural context of their countries while taking due account of the European dimension and of international requirements;
- to help higher education institutions use quality assurance techniques as steering mechanisms to promote organizational flexibility for permanent improvement in a rapidly changing environment;
- to underpin European and world-wide cooperation in order to benefit from each other's experience for the accomplishment of the two foregoing tasks.

The statement went on to recommend that quality systems should be based on a number of principles, namely autonomy and independence of the bodies responsible for quality assessment and quality assurance; relating evaluation procedures to the profile of institutions while respecting their autonomy; internal and external procedural elements; involvement of all the players; publication of evaluation reports (European Commission, 1997).

These recommendations reflected the practices and rhetoric of the existing European quality agencies which had been established at the start of the decade or before. They set an orthodoxy of practice to which later successors to quality procedures could adhere. Although it is not mandatory on member states, the EU recommendation exerts pressure 'to do something about quality' and indeed is explicit about the 'somethings' which should be done.

The statement by the European Union was based both on the experiences of the early established quality agencies and on the results of a series of pilot evaluations which a consortium of the agencies had undertaken on behalf of the EU during the first half of the decade (Thune and Staropoli, 1997). It was thus an agency/EU initiative rather than one based on any systematic views of either member governments or higher education institutions. It is worth reflecting, however, that this significant set of recommendations was based on the experiences of agencies, most of which had only been operating for a few years themselves, and that the impact of their operation had scarcely been investigated and the long-term impact not at all. The recommendations were informed neither by research on how students learn nor by the study of how higher education institutions adapt and change. The EU 'model' is now directing developments in central and eastern Europe where it is being adopted largely for reasons to do with political accession to the European Union.

Complementing, and to some extent rivalling, the EU initiatives on quality has been a programme of institutional evaluations carried out across Europe by the Association of European Universities (CRE). Mirroring the reactions of several national university bodies to public concerns about quality, the CRE initiative attempted to recognize these concerns and to accept the accountability issues which they raised without eroding existing levels of university authority over quality issues. The CRE programme now covers most parts of Europe, frequently operating alongside national systems (Barblan, 1997).

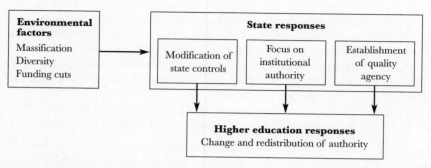

Figure 3.2 National contexts for the emergence of quality management and assessment

A political problem

Several commentators have noted that the emergence of quality assessment does not appear to have been caused by evidence of serious quality problems in higher education (e.g. Trow, 1994a and 1994b). The emergence of quality agencies is at least in part due to political problems connected with the control of higher education at a time of expansion and change. That educational problems exist and are harshly experienced in higher education institutions in many parts of the world cannot be denied, but the solutions which are being sought may have more to do with solving the political problems than the educational. Figure 3.2 attempts to summarize the changes occurring at national system levels which are giving rise to the emergence of quality assessment systems. Environmental factors which are acting directly upon institutions are also responsible for state responses which, in their turn, make further demands on institutions. The creation of national quality agencies is one feature of these state responses.

Types of quality agency

A recent survey of quality agencies in Europe identified 29 such agencies of which 15 were described as having an 'independent' legal status. However, 20 of the 29 agencies received most or all of their funding from the state (Frazer, 1997). As 'buffer organizations' between higher education and the state, a strong degree of independence may be necessary to the operational success of these agencies. Yet whatever the form of their legal status and source of funding, in nearly all cases it has been governmental concerns and agendas which have been the driving force behind the establishment of quality agencies. Even where the initiative behind the setting up of the agency has come from higher education, such moves have usually been pre-emptive and defensive attempts to avoid government setting up their own agencies.[4] In any case, the meaning and significance of terms such as 'independence' differ between countries and traditions. In reality, governments in many European countries are intimately involved in the governance of higher education in all sorts of ways and it should come as no surprise to find them involved in quality management as well.

In Mexico, since 1990, there has been a clear governmental decision to introduce quality assessment in the relationship between higher education institutions and government. This has entailed: (1) the adoption of quality criteria, (2) the creation of quality assessment agencies, (3) the creation of a National Registry of Excellent Programmes, and (4) the creation of a special Public Fund to give additional financial support to institutions on the basis of particular projects for modernizing institutions. Project proposals are assessed by ad hoc peer committees. Some of the agencies have an independent legal status from government but are funded by it, although it has to be said that assessment is carried out mainly by peers appointed by the government in agreement with the institutions.

In Australia, quality issues have come to the fore as part of the Commonwealth Government's concern to establish a greater role in the steerage of the higher education system. A number of government-sponsored quality initiatives occurred during the 1990s and these had direct links to the funding of institutions. However, state involvement in quality management in Australia has not so far been accompanied by the establishment of semi-permanent structures in the form of a national quality agency or assessment methodology (Massaro, 1997).

In considering types of quality agency, it is worth referring to the practice within several European countries of mounting pilot evaluation schemes prior to the establishment of a formal quality structure. For example, the Norwegian Institute for Studies in Research and Higher Education undertook evaluations in all Norwegian universities before a national system was established. Finland was another country which had obtained considerable experience of quality management prior to the establishment of the Finnish Higher Education Evaluation Council. The experience of these countries inevitably raises the question of whether national quality assessment necessarily requires the existence of a national quality agency, a point to which we shall return in later chapters.

Where agencies exist, they differ in terms of their legal status and sources of funding but they nearly all seek legitimacy for their activities through the participation of senior academics in their governing councils and committees, as well as co-opting the academic profession as a whole in their evaluation activities. Thus, in practice, quality agencies frequently constitute a (sometimes uneasy) alliance between higher education and the state, with the latter in the background setting limits and controls on the operation of the agency but not getting involved in its activities.

We have already noted the tensions which exist in the purposes of quality agencies and, in particular, between the most frequently mentioned purposes of improvement and accountability. However, in reviewing the statements of purpose cited in 12 quality agencies as part of the IMHE study, we identified ten purposes as follows:

- to ensure accountability for the use of public funds;
- to improve the quality of higher education provision;

- to inform funding decisions;
- to inform students and employers;
- to stimulate competitiveness within and between institutions;
- to undertake a quality check on new (sometimes private) institutions;
- to assign institutional status;
- to support the transfer of authority between the state and institutions;
- to assist mobility of students;
- to make international comparisons.

Most agencies refer to three or four of the purposes from the above list. The combination reflects national circumstances, for example the size of the country, the extent of geographical and political isolation, the extent of the marketization of higher education.

We will consider the actual consequences of quality management and assessment in later chapters, but the nature of the intended consequences needs to be referred to here. Agencies differ in the extent to which they themselves possess powers over institutions, in the extent to which there are clear mechanisms through which they can affect the decisions of other central authorities, and in the extent to which they produce information directly useful to institutions or to students and/or employers. The accreditation systems being established in many parts of eastern Europe are examples of the first of these, with direct consequences for institutions' 'licence to practice'. Both the Netherlands and Denmark have mechanisms by which the decisions of government can be directly influenced, by the Inspectorate in the case of the Netherlands and by subject committees in the case of Denmark. Most systems seek to inform wider publics through the publication of evaluation reports although the British practice of assigning numerical grades is not common elsewhere. Virtually all agencies aim to generate changes within institutions, through both the processes of evaluation and the recommendations contained in their reports.

Quality assessment is thus intended to have consequences. Whether the actual consequences are the same as the intended ones will be the subject of later chapters.

Conclusion

The degree of emphasis which is placed on accountability/control functions of quality assessment rather than improvement/change functions has differed between countries and has changed with time. Perhaps it is rather too cynical to suggest that an improvement function is stressed in order to gain support for the introduction of quality assessment systems and that an accountability function becomes more important once the system is established, although some support for this view might be found in the recent experiences of the United Kingdom, France and the Netherlands. What seems less controversial, however, is the widespread acceptance of accountability as a central feature of higher education's relationship to the state and society and the important role that quality management and assessment has in helping to provide that accountability. Frazer, for example, has emphasized accountability as the other side – and inevitable consequence – of institutional autonomy in higher education (Frazer, 1997).

There are, however, alternative positions which can be taken. For example, Trow has suggested 'trust' and 'markets' as providing alternative foundations for relationships between the state and higher education (Trow, 1996). Becher and Kogan have pointed to several different and potentially conflicting modes of accountability: the public contractual, the professional and the consumerist (Becher and Kogan, 1992: 169–70). These modes relate not only to the accountability of higher education to external interests but also, as Becher and Kogan indicate, to internal institutional decision-making processes. For example, the public contractual mode is intimately connected with what we described in Chapter 2 as 'management values'. Thus,

> In the managerial mode different levels are held together by the strongest form of relationship; namely, that of subordinates to superiors. Subsystems are committed to the pursuit of collective objectives set down for the system by the centre. Performance is rewarded and punished according to the degree of success in achieving the collective goals . . . In such cases, there is assumed to be no conflict of value, a high degree of conformity about requisite technical content, and a clear programme of tasks that must be performed.
>
> (Becher and Kogan, 1992: 169–70)

Professional accountability, in contrast, makes exogenous criteria subservient to those of 'inherent quality and to the ability to adapt expert knowledge to the individual nature of the task to be performed' (Becher and Kogan, 1992: 170). Professional accountability, according to Becher and Kogan, tends to lack 'deference to social and public needs' (p. 170).

In the case of market accountability, institutional imperatives will be set neither by government nor by academics but 'by the negotiations and quid pro quo set in a competition which is fed by public funds but which operates as a market' (Becher and Kogan, 1992: 171). Thus, as well as a distinction between accountability and improvement, we must also recognize the existence of several different modes of accountability, reflecting different interests and different values. If national quality agencies – at least within Europe – have mainly occupied ground between higher education and the state, quality management issues for institutions have to reflect an increasingly wide range of external pressures where market competition plays an important role alongside governmental and academic/collegial interests. These are among the contextual issues facing higher education institutions to which we turn in the next chapter.

Notes

1. Several sociological studies have elaborated this point through investigation of the privileges and prospects of graduates, e.g. Kelsall *et al.*, 1970; Bourdieu, 1996.
2. At the time of writing, the German Rectors Conference is proposing to establish a federal system roughly based on Dutch lines.
3. More recently, the same has come to be true of several of the countries of eastern Europe where state controls were dismantled with the fall of the Communist governments.
4. The creation of an 'academic audit unit' by the UK universities in the early 1990s and the establishment of the Association of Dutch Universities (Vereniging van Samenwerkende Nederlandse Universiteiten – VSNU) evaluation system in the Netherlands may be regarded as unsuccessful and successful 'defensive' initiatives respectively.

4

Changing Institutional Contexts: Autonomy and Accountability

Introduction

Many of the changing contexts facing higher education institutions have already been suggested by the features of the changes at the national levels described in Chapter 3. Thus, institutions have faced the consequences of growth, diversity and cuts in funding levels. Diversification has involved changes in function, in programmes, and in students. Cuts in funding levels have brought with them new funding formulae and criteria and, in many countries, a diversification of funding sources. And, of course, the establishment of national quality agencies has required a response from institutions. The common element in all of this has been the need for institutional change. In few higher education institutions around the world has the maintenance of the status quo been a realistic option, even though there are usually strong institutional forces in favour of it.

As we noted in Chapter 3, one of the most common trends at national levels has been a new emphasis upon institutional autonomy linked to new conceptions of accountability. The consequence of the former is that institutions are faced with a need to make decisions on matters which had previously been decided elsewhere. Greater autonomy, when coupled with increases in institutional diversity, implies a need to make choices about the kind of institution you are and want to become. Greater accountability reaches into the private inner lives of higher education institutions. It demands new kinds of information and new approaches to management. It changes relationships within institutions as much as it changes relationships between institutions and external agents.

In this chapter, we consider some of the characteristics of individual higher education institutions which cause them to respond differently to the forms of quality assessment confronting them. We distinguish between public and private characteristics of institutions and the various ways in which quality management is part of wider processes of institutional change. We go on to explore the diversity of institutional contexts through an examination of six of the IMHE case studies.

Differences between institutions

Just as national contexts vary considerably, so do institutional contexts. Many differences between institutions are a function of differences in national systems, but others reflect characteristics of the individual higher education institution. We will discuss some of the main lines of difference below before providing some specific examples from the case studies undertaken for the IMHE study. The point to make in all of this is that institutional contexts differ, are subject to change, and influence the nature and the scale of the impact of quality assessment.

In the first place, higher education institutions differ significantly in terms of size, mission and reputation. In the second, they also differ in their histories and traditions, in their internal organization and decision-making, and in their internal cultures. The first set of characteristics may be considered to be largely *public* features of an institution; the second set to be largely *private* features. We consider each in turn.

The public feature of the greatest concern to most higher education institutions is their reputation, their public standing. As well as being important in its own right, this is important for instrumental reasons: to attract funding, students, good staff. Reputation is largely pre-set by factors over which the institution may have little control in the short term. Antiquity is important, as is size and location (like football teams, universities located in major cities receive some of the spin-off fame of the city). Reputation within the academic community is a function of rather different factors from those affecting general reputation. To a great extent it is the aggregate of the reputations gained by an institution's departments and other basic units. But overall characteristics, particularly concerning research funding, are also important. Reputation breeds off itself. A good reputation is an excellent basis for future success. A good reputation can exist for many years after the factors responsible for it have largely disappeared. But reputation can also be damaged and a critical external assessment is something which has the potential to inflict major damage.

With diversity has come an emphasis on institutional mission. In smaller elite systems of higher education, institutions scarcely had need to articulate a mission: it was assumed that everyone knew what they did and what they were for. In mass systems, institutional diversity and mission statements provide the potential for alternative reputational criteria. Reputational claims based on extending access, on innovation, on links with industry are alternatives to traditional claims based on antiquity, prowess in research, or general academic excellence. And they have the advantage that they can be aspired to by an institution in the relatively short term. The extent to which alternative reputational criteria can successfully challenge traditional hierarchies differs between countries. Formal or informal groupings of institutions around a shared mission are increasingly common, particularly in the more market-oriented systems. Diversity of mission poses challenges for external quality assessment. Against what criteria should the institution be judged? Who is to be regarded as competent to do the judging? How can concerns about national levels of quality and standards be squared with the promotion of diversity?

In many countries, mission diversity is formally organized into different higher education sectors: *fachhochschulen* and universities in Germany, *hogescholen* and universities in the Netherlands, and a multiplicity of sectors and categories in France. In such systems, the sector in which the institution is located will itself be a crucial determinant of the character and reputation of the individual institution. Status allocation in multi-sector systems of higher education is frequently a responsibility, at least in part, of the national quality agency. Several of the newly established quality and accreditation bodies in eastern Europe perform this role as does the Quality Assurance Agency in the United Kingdom.

With the potential power to influence public perceptions of the success of higher education institutions, quality agencies provide a threat to the maintenance of existing reputations as well as the promise to enhance future reputations. The tendency for news media to convert the results of quality assessments into national league tables strengthens their potential impact. It would seem to follow that institutions with high reputations have more to lose from the results of quality assessment while institutions with lower reputations have more to gain.[1] However, as we shall see, reputation also affects the process of quality assessment, the attitudes taken to it by academic leaders and managers, and the legitimacy with which it is regarded by academic staff.

The size of an institution is likely to be associated with its reputation and mission as well as having effects on the private characteristics of the institution. Large institutions are publicly more visible. With size comes heterogeneity and organizational fragmentation. It becomes difficult to assess the whole institution in any meaningful way. In some countries, the faculties of large institutions exercise the responsibilities normally held at the centre in smaller institutions. Approaches to and impact of quality assessment are likely to be local rather than institution-wide in larger, complex institutions.

Turning to the private characteristics of higher education institutions, many of them are a reflection of their public characteristics. As we have already noted, internal fragmentation and devolution of decision-making is often associated with size. Reputations of basic units and individual professors which are achieved externally can be the basis of power and influence internally. Institutional missions which extend beyond rhetoric should impact upon organization and culture throughout the institution.

There are other private characteristics of institutions and their basic units which will affect their response to quality assessment. At the level of the basic unit, staff cohesion and relationships are likely to be important. Most forms of quality assessment require collective action from staff. The stronger the existing relationships between staff groups, the greater their capacity to produce a successful collective response to the requirements of quality assessment.

The style and approach to management at all levels in the institution is another significant factor. The importance with which quality assessment is regarded within an institution, the kinds of internal quality systems that are introduced and the extent to which they are implemented consistently across the institution will be determined largely by the attitudes of institutional and departmental managers.

Institutional histories – the saga in Burton Clark's terms (1970) – are also key determinants of culture within institutions and impose constraints on current leaders, managers and academic staff alike. The previous history of quality assessment will be particularly important. Substantial past experience can bring confidence and expertise, but it can also produce compliance, complacency and cynicism. A lack of experience can produce anxiety and even fear, but it can also bring enthusiasm and commitment.[2] In particular, previous bad experiences of quality assessment are likely to have a long-term effect on institutional attitudes. Similarly, long-standing institutional 'skeletons' may have a 'time-bomb' effect as the date of the assessment nears.

Institutional characteristics of a rather different order concern the rate and timing of institutional change. Rapid ongoing change can create difficulties for quality assessment, given the usual snapshot methodology of the assessment process (see Chapters 5 and 6). But change at least suggests that existing institutional practices are being questioned and that the questions subsequently raised are less likely to contain surprises. The absence of change makes quality assessment more straightforward; there is less scope for confusion. But the issues posed in the quality assessment process may come as a complete surprise in an institution where custom and tradition rule.

For an institution embarking on change, quality assessment can provide a useful aid to its generation and management. The IMHE case studies and other studies (e.g. Brennan, Frederiks and Shah, 1997) provide many examples of quality assessment being used as a management tool. The purpose may be to deal with a known problem, to introduce new policies or change existing structures. Whatever the management goal, quality assessment can provide an external legitimation for taking action to achieve it. The perception of an external threat can be used as an opportunity to take actions which would be otherwise unacceptable within the institution.

Martin Trow and others have drawn attention to the close association of quality assessment and so-called managerialism within higher education (Trow, 1994b). This is something which we will consider in more detail in later chapters concerned with the impact of quality assessment. However, we have already indicated our view that quality assessment frequently involves the redistribution of authority, both within institutions and between institutions and external bodies. If a general trend can be observed, it is towards the strengthening of central authority at the institutional level and the consequent weakening of authority at the levels of the state, basic units and individual academics. Even in devolved structures, authority at basic unit level is delegated from the institutional centre rather than remaining based on the collectivity of the basic unit. In other words, it is top-down rather than bottom-up. We shall consider in later chapters how different management styles interact with different methods of quality assessment to produce different outcomes. For the moment, we shall merely note that managerial authority tends to be associated with standardization of procedures and their documentation, with the existence of performance

data and its use in decision-making, with rapidity of response to external requirements, and with objectives-setting and internal accountability. The incidence of
these features of management differs between institutions and countries. The
relevance of these factors to quality assessment will be considered in Chapter 6.

So much for generalizations. The complexities of institutional cultures are
great but are of vital importance to an understanding of the part which quality
assessment plays in the generation of institutional change. In the rest of this
chapter, we describe the institutional contexts of six of the case-study institutions
from the IMHE study. We would not claim that they are necessarily typical:
indeed, we believe that the differences between them defy simple typology. They
do, however, provide illustrations of several of the points made above and are a
useful reminder of the diversity that exists in the inner lives of higher education
institutions.

Multiple evaluations and planning in a French university

Louis Pasteur University is one of France's leading scientific and medical universities. It comprises 17 separate institutional components in which some
18,000 students are enrolled. Its educational programmes are backed up by
highly developed basic research carried out in some 60 research units. The university is respected for its research achievements nationally and internationally.

The university is located in Strasbourg, close to the German and Swiss bor-
ders and home of the Council of Europe and the European Parliament. A strong
international dimension is reflected in the university's work: 14 per cent of all
students are foreign; 25 per cent of professors hired between 1991 and 1994
were foreign; 79 agreements have been signed with foreign institutions; and
there are 34 programmes under Erasmus (European Community Action
Scheme for the Mobility of University Students) agreements.

Louis Pasteur is, therefore, a university with a strong international research
reputation to maintain. But it is not immune to the kinds of changes which have
been affecting higher education in other institutions and in other countries. The
case-study authors point to the rise in student enrolments, the diversification of
programmes, the demand for vocationally oriented training and changing pedagogical practices, including the use of multimedia techniques.

Like other higher education institutions in France, Louis Pasteur University
is subject to the new policy of contracts between the central government and the
universities. This change in the relationship between higher education and the
state in France has both given institutions new autonomy and involved the
establishment of new systems of planning and assessment at national level.
These changing relations with the central state have been complemented by the
development of relations with regional socio-economic interests, relations which
have also involved regulation and assessment.

Other factors making up the context for quality assessment at Louis Strasbourg, as referred to by the case-study authors, are the university's growing

international openness and student mobility, the practice of validating acquired skills, the growth of continuing training, and the growth in competitiveness between French universities. Internally, this has led to the expansion in the range and importance of management and administrative responsibilities carried by certain academic staff. The need for planning and other administrative tools to support the work of the university's managers has become evident and quality assessment is seen as one such tool.

In the words of the authors of the case study,

> In order to have the indispensable planning tools for decision-making and for developing institutional policy and to have information that will enable it to see where it stands in relation to its national and international competitors, the Louis Pasteur University has gradually developed its quality assessment policy by combining self-evaluation with external assessment procedures carried out by outside public or private bodies. The indicators collected through these assessments are also valuable for the process of negotiating the four-year contract that defines the contractual relations between the Ministry and the university and determines for the next four years the number of posts and the financial resources provided by the central government based on the policy proposed by the university. The process of preparing this contract also provides an opportunity for stock-taking, which is a necessary step for working out this policy.
>
> (Cheminat and Hoffert, 1998: 3)

The university is subject to a range of evaluations, external and internal, and believes that these provide a useful overview of the way the university works that can be used in a variety of decision-making contexts. The case-study authors emphasize the importance of the multifaceted approach provided by a range of evaluations:

> only a combination of a variety of independent evaluations and many indicators can provide the information that the management team needs to guide its choices and identify the directions in which the university should develop.
>
> (Cheminat and Hoffert, 1998: 11)

The Louis Pasteur case study provides a number of examples of the interaction between evaluation and institutional policy. As noted, the university is subject to a variety of different evaluations. Rather than regard these as burdens, the university appears to value their existence and to be using them for its own purposes. These purposes derive both from the regulatory framework which governs relations between higher education and the state in France (e.g. the contracts system) and the university's own development needs which reflect its wish to maintain its position as a leading international research university by coping successfully with changing external circumstances.

Accountability and development at a Welsh university

Cardiff is the largest constituent institution of the Federal University of Wales, with 25 departments and schools and nearly 14,000 students. At the time that the case study was written, the university – along with the rest of UK higher education – was subject to three major forms of external quality assessment dealing respectively with teaching, research, and institutional quality assurance procedures. Many individual departments are also subject to assessment and accreditation by external professional bodies.

The university has a well-developed institutional quality policy which is described in detail within the case study. In large part it derives from the aims of the university's corporate plan, which refer to the achievement and enhancement of quality and the importance of responding to the changing needs and aspirations of students. As the case-study authors point out, it is difficult to attribute the institution's quality policy directly to the existence of external quality requirements, as it reflected needs that were present anyway. Some of these stemmed from the merger in 1988 of University College Cardiff and the University of Wales Institute of Science and Technology into the new institution. This and other changes experienced by the university reflect broader contextual developments, of which the introduction of external quality processes was also a reflection. The range of changes are described in the case-study report:

> They reflect the tremendous changes in culture within higher education itself: a heightened awareness of the use, and in some instances, the mis-use of league tables; the public's perception of higher education provision and the national and international raising of consciousness about quality in higher education institutions. The changes form part of the University's response to the 35 per cent increase in student numbers in the last 5 years, the process of modularization, and raised expectations on the part of its students.
>
> (Daniels, 1998)

Cardiff University of Wales appears to have developed quite elaborate quality mechanisms during the 1990s. Their creation reflects a mixture of concerns which include new forms of accountability and public perceptions of higher education as well as needs arising out of expansion, curriculum change and the expectations of students.

Creating a new institution in Finland

Whereas both Louis Pasteur and Cardiff are large well-established international universities seeking to maintain and extend established reputations, Vantaa Polytechnic in Finland is a new and relatively small institution actively seeking to achieve recognition and further to meet primarily regional needs.

During the 1990s, Finland was creating a non-university sector of polytechnic institutions in an experimental fashion, involving the merger of existing institutes and a licensing system based on external evaluation by the Council for the Evaluation of Higher Education. The development of the sector has been competitive insofar as existing institutes may apply for a licence to become a polytechnic. It appears that only a finite number of licences will be granted (Antikainen and Mattila,1998).

At the time that the case study was written, Vantaa Polytechnic was an institution of 1,500 students, one of 28 institutions which provide education at higher professional levels in Finland. It had applied unsuccessfully for a licence for full polytechnic status. Its current status was that of an 'experimental polytechnic'. Since the case study was written, it has expanded through mergers with eight colleges from different parts of the province of Uusimaa to become an institution of some 8,000 students. This makes it potentially Finland's largest polytechnic.

Vantaa Polytechnic is therefore in the middle of a process of institution building. Central to this will be a renewed application for a polytechnic licence, although this may be sought for different parts of the new institution in different years dependent upon their 'maturity' as assessed through internal and external evaluations.

The situation of Vantaa offers a clear illustration of the twin functions of quality assessment in (1) securing external status and (2) supporting internal development.

> Evaluation is a central tool in the development of polytechnics, as through evaluation it is possible to obtain necessary information for directing and improving all its activities. Evaluation can be said to involve a built-in demand for change. In order to obtain objective information, external evaluation is of vital importance.
>
> (Antikainen and Mattila, 1998: 10)

In the event, the polytechnic has undertaken self-evaluation, external evaluation as part of the licensing process, and further external evaluation for its own development processes.

At the time that the case study was written, a national system of external quality assessment was in the process of establishment in Finland and the methods of the new Council for the Evaluation of Higher Education were not clear. The polytechnic's experience of external evaluation as part of the licensing process had been frustrating. But the need for external evaluation as part of the polytechnic's development was emphasized by the case-study authors. In particular, they note the link between evaluation and decentralized planning.

> One of the reasons for launching major internal evaluation processes in polytechnics is the fact that a centralized educational planning system no longer exists in Finland. In a decentralized planning system the curricula are produced in each institution separately with an emphasis on local factors and synergy benefits. When an internal evaluation system for a

polytechnic is developed, the principles emphasizing local factors must be taken into account.

(Antikainen and Mattila, 1998: 10)

Departments with problems in Amsterdam

If the Vantaa case study provides a useful example of the role of quality assessment in building a new institution, the case study of the University of Amsterdam illustrates how pressures of change facing large well-established institutions can give rise to internal assessment activities. The university is a large, classical university with 14 faculties and 26,000 students. The case study examines the circumstances facing two of the university's faculties: psychology and economics. The Amsterdam case study is one of the most open and honest descriptions of the problems which a major university faced.

The case-study authors describe the situation in the university's psychology faculty as follows:

> In the early 1990s, the Faculty of Psychology had many educational problems, including a tremendous increase in student enrolment that climaxed with 750 first-year students in 1992, a major decline in progression and yields, severe student dissatisfaction with the programme's massive and impersonal nature and the aloofness among the staff, complaints about the level of many examinations, poor curriculum content, unsatisfactory course capacity, a flawed student administration, badly co-ordinated information for prospective students, mediocre information for enrolled students, little systematic educational evaluation and no follow-up, and so on. Students felt unwanted and deplored the qualitative deficiencies (if only the instructors were better, if only they received better guidance, etc) while instructors attributed all problems both to an excessively large student body and to the lack of motivation (there are too many students, their standards are too low, they are lazy, etc).

(de Klerk *et al.*, 1998: 11)

This graphic description might strike a cord of familiarity with readers in many other large universities. The case study goes on to describe the steps that were taken by the faculty to rectify the situation. These involved both self-assessment and active follow-up. Real problems clearly had existed and internal assessment processes played a vital part in rectifying them.

It must also be noted, however, that a few years previously the psychology faculty had undergone a trial external assessment carried out by an external committee of the Association of Dutch Universities (Vereniging van Samenwerkende Nederlandse Universiteiten – VSNU). The VSNU has been carrying out subject-level assessments of Dutch universities since the late 1980s. This early one appears to have had little penetration. The case-study authors write that the faculty regarded it as a bureaucratic operation that required co-operation. Of the report they write:

The friendly and favourable (and above all confidential) report contained few points of criticism and focused on several more organizational and procedural matters. In effect, the assessment and its findings were of little importance to the Faculty.

(de Klerk *et al.*, 1998: 11)

To be fair to the VSNU assessment system, an assessment of psychology at the University of Amsterdam a few years later seems to have been more penetrating and more useful to the university. But the second assessment took place at a time when quality issues were high on the agenda of the faculty. The external assessment had not put them there. They reflected real problems which the faculty wished to address.

The case study of economics at the University of Amsterdam illustrates a very different kind of scenario. An external assessment carried out in 1990 had been very critical: the curriculum, the educational support, the programme's didactic quality, the development of faculty-wide educational policy, were all considered below average. Yet this critical external report does not appear to have led directly to action within the faculty. This is not because the criticisms were disputed. Rather, according to the case-study authors, 'A crisis within the faculty administration caused the negative educational assessment to fade into the background' (de Klerk *et al.*, 1998: 16).

An internal university investigation into the nature and causes of this crisis produced a report that was even more critical than the external assessment had been. Research quality was criticized, educational processes and structures were regarded as unsatisfactory. Cultural and management factors were deemed to be the major cause of the serious problems faced by the faculty.

The lack of social cohesion within the faculty was identified as a major determinant of the crisis situation: 'the organization does not operate as a community in terms of a group of people linked by a common mission statement and a common culture.' Internally, the faculty is found to be divided along the lines of the various departments. Externally, the faculty was characterized by a very hostile attitude toward the university's central administration for its perceived financial discrimination against the faculty.

(de Klerk *et al.*, 1998: 16)

The authors of the case study describe how gradual but effective actions were taken by the faculty and the university to address the problems which had been identified both externally and internally. A further internal assessment in 1995 by the faculty board was able to conclude that 'The faculty is now under firm administration and has a professional bureau with orderly operations and totally redesigned curricula to be introduced in the next academic year' (de Klerk *et al.*,1998: 16).

The Amsterdam case study reminds us that even the largest, most prestigious universities can have real and serious quality problems but that they can generate the will and the capacity to do something about them. In the Amsterdam case, the external assessments appear to have been of relatively little importance. We should not assume, however, that this will always be the case. Nor should we assume that quality problems in universities are always identified and acted upon internally. The case-study authors emphasize the importance of the institutional context as a key variable influencing the effectiveness of quality assessment:

> the ideal assessment and response is attainable only in a quiet, friction-less world where external assessment is the only relevant factor. In reality, how-ever, external assessment is but one of several factors influencing institu-tional development.
>
> (de Klerk *et al.*, 1998: 17)

This might suggest that external assessment is least efficacious in the circum-stances which need it most. However, such a conclusion would be premature. Higher education institutions are capable of dealing with their own problems but they may need a stimulus to do so; and sometimes this might come from external quality assessment. However, there are other factors which can pro-voke change within universities. External assessment is not always effective in this respect, especially if the institutional context is not receptive to it.

Quality assessment in the highly regulated Italian context

The case-study report of Ca'Foscari University of Venice is interesting because the institution had, in recent years, introduced an internal system of quality assessment even though Italy did not possess a national quality assessment system. The university also chose to participate in the international institutional quality assessment programme of the Association of European Universities (CRE).

The institutional context in the case of Ca'Foscari is one of considerable recent growth, major funding shortages, and complex decision-making struc-tures. Within a 10- to 12-year period the university population of Venice increased by about 70 per cent to around 19,000 students in 1995. The stu-dent–staff ratio of the university is 56.5 students per teacher compared with a national figure of 29.8. The ratio of non-teaching staff to students is similarly high with one staff member for every 44 students compared with a national aver-age of one to 25. Very substantial overcrowding of lectures is only avoided because large numbers of students do not turn up for them. Hardly any students complete their studies within the scheduled time. A principle of democratic rep-resentation in all decision-making structures ensures that decisions are always taken collectively. Decisions are virtually never delegated to a single person.

The university provides an example of a classic European situation of a com-bination of detailed state regulations with traditions of maximum autonomy for individual professors. The state decides on overall subject curricula and professors decide on what specifically to teach: 'the University has little control over curricula (because of centralized control) and over syllabus (because of professors' freedom)' (Warglein and Savoia, 1998: 9).

The university also has little control over staffing in terms of either who to hire or what to require of them. By law, a professor must teach at least one course a year (72 hours) but there is little incentive to teach more than this minimum. There is similarly limited authority over research activity and research performances are not checked: 'The career development is the only reason for research and publishing. However, given that the promotions are not controlled at the university level, the institution has no control over this process' (p. 10). The authors of the case study summarize the constraints faced by their university as lack of financial resources, limits of space, national restrictions on the recruitment of teaching and non-teaching staff, national restrictions on the opening of new study programmes, and limitations imposed by the decision-making structure of the university (p. 11).

Faced with these constraints and rigidities, it is not easy to see what quality assessment could be expected to achieve. But the national context of higher education in Italy is gradually beginning to change, together with the accompanying funding mechanisms. The financial act of 1994 introduced a single all-inclusive transfer payment from the ministry to the university in place of an aggregate of purposive and non-alterable transfer payments. The new kind of grant has no constraints and the university is allowed to allocate resources according to its own priorities. The ministry has also given universities freedom to raise tuition fees to students and, at the time that the case study was written, consideration was being given to changing the method of financing from one based on past expenditure to a method based on levels of activities (essentially student numbers) and levels of efficiency. Other changes at a national level, coupled with the university's desire to develop both its regional and its international roles, have helped to set the context for the introduction of quality assessment.

The introduction of quality assessment at Ca'Foscari appears to have been partly a decision to help the university exploit the slightly greater flexibility offered by changes in the national context, i.e. the beginnings of deregulation. However, it is also noted in the case study that the creation of the university's Internal Evaluation Unit was intended to meet the requirements of two national laws. Evaluation at Ca'Foscari appears to be largely about the improvement of efficiency. In time it might be the precursor to the exercise of a greater degree of managerialism in the university. However, at the time that the case study was written, the authors note that evaluation was having little impact on internal decision-making. Given the complexities of decision-making structures, the finding seems hardly surprising. The Evaluation Unit was attempting to tie its future activities to issues of strategic management of the university in an attempt to increase its usefulness for decision-making.

Quality assessment for increased productivity in Mexico

From a case study in a highly regulated higher education system we turn to a case study set in a country where a large degree of legal autonomy for universities has been traditional for most of this century. In Mexico, public universities have very broad freedom both to determine their academic policies and to control the financial resources which they receive from the state. The latter are negotiated directly by means of informal relationships between universities and educational authorities.

The Autonomous Metropolitan University (Universidad Autónoma Metropolitana – UAM) in Mexico City is a large institution with some 40,000 students. It is also a distinctive institution. It was founded in 1968 following student unrest in that period. It sought to provide an alternative university model which addressed some of the criticisms that had been made by the students. Its distinctive features included its decentralization, operating on three largely self-governing campuses; a very high composition of full-time professors (in contrast to the large proportion of part-time staff to be found in other Mexican universities); and a departmental organizational structure which aimed to promote a close relationship between teaching and research. The university has a collegiate form of government. Because of its many innovative features – and not least the political circumstances surrounding its creation – UAM has enjoyed comparatively favourable levels of state funding from its inception.

However, economic crises in Mexico during the 1980s led to a sharp drop in the funding of all public universities. This especially affected the wages of academics and administrative personnel.

> This coincided with a time in which the social usefulness of public spending was being questioned by some intellectuals and economists, and sometimes even by governments of different countries. The cutbacks caused many academics to abandon public universities in order to work in the government, the private sector or in the private universities, which in this period registered a notable growth and were able to pay competitive wages to their personnel. Other academics remained in the public universities, but their commitment to their work was lessened as most were forced to take on second jobs to supplement their income.
>
> (Valenti and Varela, 1998: 5)

At the end of the 1980s, the country's economic situation improved and this brought budgetary increases for higher education. These were, however, conditional and applied selectively. New funds to higher education have been regarded as 'extraordinary payments' on top of ordinary wages.

> Thus, starting in 1989–90, progressively, pay increases for academic personnel follow a double logic: on one hand, normal increases to the basic wages that respond to the restrictions created by the government's anti-inflationary economic policy; and on the other, increases by way of special

incentives for productivity which in some institutions, including the UAM, can add between 100 and 200 per cent to the basic wage. This second income is granted variably as a reflection of the annual productivity of each individual, according to concrete quality assessment mechanisms that vary in each institution of higher education.

(Valenti and Varela, 1998: 6)

The Mexican government has also established a national system of quality assessment in higher education run by the National Commission for Higher Education (Comisión Nacional de Evaluación de la Educación Superior – CONAEVA) which operates at three operational levels: institutional self-assessment, quality assessment of academic programmes by peer review committees, and quality assessment of the higher education system as a whole by CONAEVA. Note however that

The fulfilment by the higher education institutions of the requirements of information resulting from self-assessment influences the educational authorities' decisions on the allocation of funding, and the peer review committees (called CIEES) provide inputs in order to improve the quality of programmes.

(Valenti and Varela, 1998: 6)

This reverses the more usual idea that self-assessment is mainly about improvement and external assessment is mainly about accountability and/or allocation.

In this context, the incentives for UAM to develop an effective internal system of quality assessment are clear. The credibility of its own assessment system would enhance its claims for increased state funding as well as reduce the case for intrusive external assessment. It could also offer a route to wage increases for academic staff, thus reducing the opposition to assessment found in other places. The success of the policy would also contribute to the university's competitiveness, both within Mexican higher education and internationally:

this position (by UAM) involved reaching a pragmatic agreement with the government allowing the university to take the quality assessment mechanism into its own hands, thus avoiding the possibility that some other mechanism that the university had not designed and did not control would be imposed. This coincided with the emphasis on one of the three levels of quality assessment defined by the CONAEVA, the level which, in fact, has operated with the most efficiency to date, that of university self assessment. At the same time, this implied giving up the possibility of rejecting quality assessment on the basis of the rhetorical defence of the legal autonomy of the public universities, an option that would have also effectively closed off the possibility of obtaining new state financing.

(Valenti and Varela, 1998: 7)

The quality assessment system at UAM operates at both individual and unit levels and involves substantial financial rewards for each (see Chapter 5). This has no doubt led to productivity improvements across the university as well as to the desired effect of achieving a favourable financial deal with the ministry.

Conclusion: a need to comply and a need to change

These six examples of institutional contexts for quality assessment are illustrative of the considerable differences which exist across the 29 case studies undertaken for the IMHE study. In part, these differences reflect national system characteristics, but in all cases they are mediated by more local circumstances and strategies at the level of the individual institution.

Although changes in state policies on higher education play a part in most cases, such policies do not seem to be the most decisive factors in the introduction of institutional quality systems. The appearance of a national quality agency is but one consideration among many that determine institutional approaches to quality. Other and perhaps more important factors include cuts in funding, deregulation, binary policies, expansion and increased competition. Most institutions face a need to manoeuvre themselves to respond successfully to the opportunities and threats present in the external environment, whether these concern state policies and funding and/or competitive advantage over other institutions. Many institutions, or parts of institutions, face real problems – including, in some cases, poor management – to which internal quality assessment may promise to provide solutions.

Higher education institutions face two different kinds of problem: the need to comply with changing external requirements and the need to initiate changes to deal with internal problems which may themselves be partly created by changes in the external environment. The need to comply is not just about accountability to the state. Failure to do so can affect institutional reputation and, with it, market competitiveness. The need to change creates a challenge to existing decision-making structures and brings the possibility of a redistribution of authority within the institution.

The large variations which exist in institutional contexts make it difficult to predict the effects of the introduction of quality assessment in any particular institution and make it desirable to adapt assessment methods to the context of the institution. The extent to which this is possible depends in part upon the characteristics of the external assessment system. The relationship between external and internal quality assessment methods is the subject of the next two chapters.

Notes

1. A contention supported by the results of a study of the impact of quality assessment in England (Brennan, Frederiks and Shah, 1997).
2. These and other observations are based on the results of studies of the impact of quality assessment (e.g. Frederiks *et al.*, 1994; Brennan *et al.*, 1996; Bauer and Henkel, 1998) as well as the IMHE case studies.

5

The Methods of Quality Agencies

Introduction

National quality agencies face a variety of problems, not least that of achieving acceptability and credibility with the higher education community on the one hand and with the state on the other. Other common problems arise from the size and diversity of the higher education systems which they are attempting to assess, the culture and traditions of individual institutions and the extent and forms of regulatory mechanisms to which they are subject.

In a review of the evaluation systems in a mostly different set of countries from those which are the focus of this book, Cowen reports that

> Governments are looking at what other governments are doing in the evaluation of higher education systems and, through various networks, are establishing contacts, arranging seminars for policy makers and adapting well or poorly the foreign evaluation policies which interest them.
>
> (Cowen, 1996: 3)

Governments are helped in these enterprises by various international organizations. In Europe, the European Union has published guidelines and sponsored pilot assessments (Thune and Staropoli, 1997); the CRE (Association of European Universities) promotes its own programme of institutional-level reviews (Barblan, 1997); the Council of Europe and UNESCO have also supported activities related to assessment themes (European Commission, 1998); and the OECD–IMHE has supported work on performance indicators (Kells, 1993) as well as the project on which much of this book is based.

A model which has been influential in many parts of the world has been the US system of accreditation, established since the beginning of the century. The US accreditation agencies, therefore, have some claim to be the forerunners of the quality agencies which have been established in the 1990s. Yet during this decade, the US agencies have themselves been subject to considerable debate and some criticisms (e.g. Dill, 1997; El-Khawas, 1998). As one critic has put it,

To a considerable extent, external academic accountability in the United States, mainly in the form of accreditation, has been irrelevant to the improvement of higher education; in some cases it has acted more to shield institutions from effective monitoring of their own educational performance than to provide it; in still other cases it distinctly hampers the efforts of institutions to improve themselves.

(Trow, 1996: 7)

However irrelevant they might be to the inner lives of higher education institutions, the accreditation bodies can of course help to provide an external legitimacy to the work of these institutions. That might be their main intent although, as we noted in Chapter 3, many quality agencies profess a wide range of purposes among which institutional and educational improvement generally figure prominently. Indeed, much of the debate about the methods (as opposed to the politics) of quality agencies has been about whether the same methods can achieve both accountability and improvement or, in the terminology of the evaluation literature, be both summative and formative (Kogan, 1986). Commentators such as Trow suggest that the combination cannot be obtained (Trow, 1996) while others argue that an appropriate balance of formative and summative assessment can and must be achieved (Vroeijenstijn, 1994). Still other writers appear to 'wish away' summative assessment and accountability issues and place virtually all their emphasis upon improvement goals (e.g. Barnett, 1992; Taylor, 1994).

Most of the European countries represented in the IMHE study had been influenced by the ideas contained in a 'general model' of quality assessment, supported and promoted by the European Union and based on a review sponsored by the EU at the start of the decade. The review was carried out by Dutch researchers (van Vught and Westerheijden, 1993) who had very little European experience to draw on at the time: only the British and French had reasonably well-established national assessment systems (and the former was experiencing major changes) and the Dutch had fairly recently set up a system of their own. The proposed model was influenced by this experience and also by US accreditation systems. It appears to have been influential in shaping developments in Europe during the rest of the decade and we will use it as a framework in which to describe the methods of the quality agencies which existed in the participating countries in the IMHE study.

The next section of this chapter describes the main elements of the model. In the subsequent section, we look at some of the variations which exist between the methods used by national quality agencies and consider the extent to which the model can indeed be regarded as having general applicability. In the final section, we consider in more detail the methods used by quality agencies in three countries, two of which (the Netherlands and Denmark) accord quite closely to the general model, while the third (Mexico) represents a separate and rather different approach. The descriptions of and references to the various methods of quality assessment described in this chapter are those that were in operation at the time that the case studies were prepared, mainly by the agencies themselves, for the IMHE study. Some of the details are likely to have changed since.

Quality assessment model

The 'general model' proposed by the European Union and others based on the review undertaken by van Vught and Westerheijden (1993) has four main elements:

1. *A national body* with responsibility for co-ordinating and setting out the procedures and methods to be used by institutions of higher education for the assurance of quality. Such a body should, according to the model, have legal status but be independent of government.

The detailed operational aspects of the national body would vary according to the *level and focus* of quality assessment. These would, in turn, have an effect on the next three elements:

2. Based on the procedures and methods set out by the national co-ordinating body, institutions should undertake regular *self-evaluation* and report to the co-ordinating body on a regular basis. For this process to be effective, the self-evaluation should be undertaken by the academic staff of the institution themselves.
3. The institutional self-evaluation would form the basis of an *external peer evaluation*. Such an evaluation should include discussions with academic and administrative staff, students and alumni. The external peers would need to be selected to represent specific expertise (academic, management, etc) depending on the focus and purpose of the visit.
4. *A published report* setting out the findings of the peer review visit should be made. The main purpose of the report should be to make recommendations to institutions in order to help them improve the quality of their teaching and research.

Accordingly, the model seems to assume that the predominant purpose of quality assessment is improvement. A fifth element of the model in its earlier versions – that there should be no direct link between the outcomes of quality assessment and the funding of institutions – was in line with this improvement emphasis. The inclusion, however, of this fifth element, couched in a negative formulation, appears to be a somewhat defensive recognition of the other purposes, less benign in the eyes of academe, to which quality assessment could be put.

As noted above, this model resulted from a study undertaken for the Commission of the European Communities in 1991 of the methods of quality assessment used in the member states and in certain other countries, notably the United States. The Standing Conference of Rectors, Presidents and Vice-Chancellors of the European universities were consulted. The study highlighted a growing interest in the member states in quality assurance in higher education.

At this time the Commission felt that 'quality in an increasingly diversified higher education was an issue of paramount importance . . . merely evaluating the scientific quality of research and staff is no longer a guarantee as to the quality of teaching . . .' (European Commission, 1997). The Commission has, since the mid-1990s, promoted this model not just in the member states but also in central and eastern Europe. In particular, it has supported pilot assessments based on the model, particularly in those countries – east and west – which had not at the time established a national quality system (Thune and Staropoli, 1997; EC PHARE, 1998a).

The 'general model' has been especially influential in developments throughout Europe; the quality assessment methods of most established and developing agencies include the four main elements of the model. It also appears to be compatible with the well-established accreditation system in the United States. It is less clear, however, whether the model is particularly helpful or applicable to developments in other parts of the world, for example in Mexico or, to a lesser extent, in Australia. In Mexico there are several different agencies and levels of evaluation. In Australia, a Committee for Quality Assurance in Higher Education (CQAHE) was set up in 1992 as a non-statutory ministerial advisory committee to review and verify at institutional level structures and procedures for quality assurance in three areas (teaching and learning, research, and community service) over a three-year cycle. Institutions were asked to produce 'quality portfolios' in accordance with a prescribed formula from the CQAHE for each of the areas. These quality portfolios formed the basis of institutional claims for additional funding. However, a change of government resulted in the early discontinuation of these arrangements.

While this 'general model' appears on the surface to be fairly widely applicable, there are many variations and differences in the methods used. These include the range and types of national bodies, the level and focus of assessment, the purposes of self-evaluation, the types of external peers used and their selection and training, the types of reports, to whom they are addressed, and who follows them up. They also differ in the consequences that result from the evaluations and how they affect decision-making in the national higher education system. Some of the major variations and differences in the main elements of the model are discussed in the next section.

Variations in methods

National bodies

The national quality assessment bodies differ from country to country in their legal status and ownership, their functions, their composition and their sources of funding. Agencies may be set up by government (for example, the Danish Centre for Evaluation and Quality Assessment), be owned collectively by the institutions (for example, the Association of Dutch Universities (Vereniging van Samenwerkende Nederlandse Universiteiten – VSNU) in the Netherlands and the former Higher Education Quality Council in the United Kingdom), or they can be independent bodies (for example, the National Evaluation Committee (Comité National d'Évaluation – CNE) in France and the Quality Assurance Agency in the United Kingdom). Whatever the formal status of the agencies, on the whole they exist because governments want them to exist and the methods they use represent a compromise between what governments want and what institutions are prepared to accept. As with many 'intermediary bodies', the agencies co-opt members of the higher education community for expertise and legitimacy (Clark, 1983) irrespective of the agency's formal status and ownership. In many countries, quality agencies are part of a wider set of arrangements for assessing and managing quality. Exclusive focus on the agency can obscure other features of the quality system. For example, the VSNU in the Netherlands is the national co-ordinating body with responsibility for undertaking the external quality assessment at programme level within the institutions but the overall evaluation and follow-up of the outcomes of the individual programme assessments is the responsibility of the Inspectorate for Higher Education which reports to the Ministry of Education. This represents an attempt to achieve neutrality and independence of evaluation by ensuring a clear separation of powers.

There is more than one meta-level agency in some countries, for example in the United States, the United Kingdom and Mexico. In the United States, quality assessment is in the form of 'accreditation'. There are two types of accreditation agencies. One is responsible for accreditation at institutional level (regional accrediting bodies) and the other is responsible for programme accreditation (specialist agencies). Specialized accreditation is carried out in programmes which prepare professionals in fields such as dentistry, engineering and law. Each specialized accreditation body has its own distinctive definitions of eligibility criteria or standards for accreditation and operating procedures. There are several agencies of both types because of the size of the country. Participation in both these levels of accreditation is voluntary but almost all institutions view it as a beneficial or politically necessary process and so opt to be accredited. Higher education in the United States is a strongly market-led system so failure to achieve accreditation can lead to a number of consequences (a major one being a loss of reputation and therefore a drop in enrolments). Until 1993, recognition of both regional and specialized accreditation agencies was vested in a national umbrella body called the Council on Post-Secondary Accreditation (COPA). With the demise of COPA national co-ordination of this multi-agency system has been a sensitive issue and several proposed mechanisms have failed to be implemented. COPA's core members were the regional accrediting groups and it was dependent on their support for its existence. The groups lost confidence in COPA's abilities to meet their needs.

In addition to this voluntary accreditation, individual states also play a role in mandatory quality assessment. This varies from state to state but can involve (1) reviews of programmes on a rolling basis according to state applied guidelines; (2) programme approval which looks mainly at inputs (e.g. faculty qualifications, existing provision and demand); and (3) performance improvement criteria which all publicly funded institutions have to meet to receive state funding.

Until recently in the United Kingdom two agencies were responsible for different levels of evaluation of teaching, research and institutional management and policy. The agency with responsibility for evaluation at the institutional level was owned by the institutions (the Higher Education Quality Council) and the agencies with responsibility for programme level evaluation and research (the funding councils) were accountable to the government to ensure that the course provision in the institutions that they funded was of appropriate quality. The latter agencies also had responsibility to ensure that value for money was achieved through greater selectivity of research funding. The quality assessment system in the United Kingdom has recently undergone major changes and, as from 1997, the functions of the quality council and the teaching quality assessment functions of the funding councils (research assessment remains a direct responsibility of the funding councils) have been brought together under the aegis of one co-ordinating body – the Quality Assurance Agency. After much consultation with appropriate groups, the Agency set out a new methodology for quality assessment which was at the time of our study being piloted (QAA, 1998). Institutions of higher education in the United Kingdom are also subject to evaluation by a range of other bodies for accreditation of qualifications for professional purposes.

In France and Mexico also, multiple systems of external assessment exist and a single co-ordinating body cannot be identified. In Germany, there is no single assessment system at national level, with operational higher educational responsibilities resting with individual Lander.

From these examples, it can be seen that the concept of a single national body does not appear to fit well with developments in several countries. In some, there are several quality assessment agencies and their functions include more than *co-ordination*: they undertake the assessment process. Higher education systems in these countries are large and diverse. Any single system of assessment encounters problems of costs and consistency in large countries. It would, therefore, appear that this element of the general model is most suited to countries with medium-sized and less diverse higher education systems.

Level and focus of assessment

National quality agencies also differ considerably in the level and focus of their assessment methods. The *level* of external assessment can be institutional, faculty/department, subject/programme or individual. The *focus* at each of these levels can be on teaching, research or management/administration. The most common levels are the subject/programme or whole institution and sometimes a combination of both (as in the case of the United Kingdom and the United States, as mentioned above, where they are subject to separate and not integrated processes). Although there has been a long tradition of evaluation of research in most countries, evaluation of teaching is a recent development which is becoming of increasing importance.

The focus of assessment at programme level usually includes structure and organization of the course, teaching and learning objectives, academic staff details, library and other learning resources, information technology, student progress and achievement, staff development and internal quality assurance mechanisms.

The focus at whole institution level varies a lot. Potentially it can deal with most of the activities of an institution from institutional systems (mission, governance, management, quality assurance, finance and physical resources), to quality of education (aims and objectives, assessment methods, student achievement, employability of graduates, research and scholarship, qualifications and experience of teaching staff, learning resources, accommodation, student support services), to quality of research (number of publications, facilities – laboratories and equipment, library and information technology – external funding, collaboration with industry). The CNE in France focuses on most of these activities. Other systems (for example institutional audit in the United Kingdom) focus on quality management aspects only. The regional accreditation systems in the United States focus mainly on financial and management issues.

Variations in levels and focus can also give rise to variations in values and criteria of assessment. Institutional-level assessment has a tendency to be 'managerial', involving a concentration on internal structures and procedures, including lines of internal accountability. Subject-level assessment is more likely to reflect disciplinary academic values, particularly when the emphasis is on research, although both pedagogic and employability values enter into the assessment of teaching to varying degrees in different systems. For example, the Danish system has placed a lot of emphasis on employment values and the UK subject-level system has taken a largely 'pedagogic approach' to teaching assessment.

Self-evaluation

The second element of the 'general model' is self-evaluation. Providing that a fairly liberal definition of the term is adopted, self-evaluation is used in the quality assessment methodology in most countries. Its main purpose is to enable the institution (or sub-unit) to provide appropriate, relevant and up-to-date information about itself. The self-evaluation usually forms the basis against which judgements can be reached by the external assessment team. In a pan-European survey of processes and policy issues of academic quality assessment and accreditation, it was found that 29 out of 30 agencies reported using a self-evaluation process as the basis for external review (Frazer, 1997).

Institutional self-evaluation is undertaken by the relevant institutional staff (usually academics) in response to the requirements of a national agency. In many of the case studies which formed part of our project, however, the institution or department itself initiated self-evaluation for other purposes. This was sometimes in anticipation of some subsequent external assessment system (for example, where an agency was planned but not yet operational) but more commonly it was in response to some internally defined problem or need. Internal assessment of this sort is the subject of Chapter 6.

The content of the self-evaluation is to some extent determined by the institution/department undertaking the activity but most national agencies tend to prescribe guidelines/frameworks or a prestructured questionnaire on which the self-evaluation should be based. The Dutch agency (VSNU) and a recently established agency in Germany (Lower Saxony) are good examples of this. In relation to the former,

> The cornerstone of the system is a self-analysis . . . of the strengths/weaknesses of the educational programme . . . and it should perform three functions:
>
> - promote processes of internal quality assurance;
> - serve as internal preparation for a visit of the (agency) review committee;
> - provide background information for the review committee.
>
> These three functions, especially the third one, necessitate a rather strict set of guidelines as to which items should be included in the self-analysis and in what way. If a review committee is to assess several educational programmes from the same discipline but from different universities, it must possess comparable information about each of the educational programmes. For this reason a set of rather strict guidelines has been prepared by the VSNU to which the self-analysis must adhere.
>
> (Zijderveld, 1997: 4)

In Lower Saxony, 'To support the self-evaluation, the quality assessment agency provides the department with a pre-structured questionnaire' (Reuke, 1997: 3).

In whatever form the information is provided, the contents of the self-evaluation reports appear to be similar but there are variations in the specifications about their length and the amount of time that institutions are given to submit them. These can, of course, affect how the process is handled by the institutions and the quality of the final report.

A key question is whether the self-evaluation is just an information-gathering exercise or whether it is a genuinely critical self-evaluation. A linked issue concerns who the self-evaluation is meant to benefit. Is it just to meet the requirements of the external agency or would it have been undertaken without any external pressure? While all agencies report problems in ensuring that self-evaluations are sufficiently 'evaluative', agencies also differ in the extent to which evaluation – as opposed to information – is actually required. The UK audit, French CNE evaluation and accreditation systems in eastern Europe are all primarily descriptive forms of 'self-evaluation'. More generally, institutions tend to find it difficult to be critical and evaluative when the results are to be used by an external evaluation group.

External peer evaluation

Peer review is a feature of the quality assessment process of virtually all national systems. It has long been used in the evaluation of research (for example, through the refereeing process of academic articles). However, it varies considerably from one system to another. The differences concern who the external peers are, what is expected of them, how they are selected, how visits are organized, the length of visits and who is seen during them (for example, are students included in the process?). These variations often relate to the authority and discretion that peers have during the process. How far are peers seen as representatives of the agency or as members of the subject-based peer groups – the wider academic community?

The main variations in the way external peer review is carried out by national agencies is set out under the following four categories: sources of authority of peers, types of peers, selection and training of peers, and the site visits. Each of these is, of course, influenced by the focus of the review (teaching, research, management, etc), the level of review (institution, department, subject, individual) and the purposes of the review (usually a combination of accountability and improvement) (Brennan *et al.*, 1994).

There are two distinct *sources of authority* among peers. The first is where the peers have 'moral' authority based on the shared membership, knowledge and values of a particular peer grouping. This is most often found at subject level and constitutes individuals with a common educational background and professional identity that, in turn, forms the basis of shared interests and loyalties. The other form of peer authority is derived from the powers of the organization on behalf of whom the peers are acting. In the latter case, the shared disciplinary values of the peer group may be subordinated to the values of the agency as a basis for the criteria to be used in the assessment process.

National agencies vary in the *types of peers* that they use. Depending on the focus and level of the review, peers are made up from a single subject group, a mixture of subject experts and the academic profession as a whole, pedagogic experts, administrators and managers in institutions, international experts, experts from industry and commerce, and also, in some cases, students. Clearly, it is difficult to see how many of these groups can be said to constitute 'peers' and, indeed, some agencies do not use 'peer' terminology to describe their visiting groups.

The status and reputation of the peers is important. Most agencies consider it important to ensure that peers are equivalent in status to those being reviewed. In an earlier study (Brennan *et al.*, 1994), we found that there were some common criteria applied by national agencies in the types of peers that they selected. These criteria varied according to the purpose of the review. For reviews at institutional level, peer groups comprised individuals with academic/educational qualifications, representatives from industry and commerce without relevant subject knowledge, and people with higher education management experience. For research reviews, individuals sought were those with relevant subject expertise from within the academic community and those with similar expertise from outside the higher education sector. Where peers were selected for their subject expertise (whether for teaching or research), priority was given to research reputation, teaching experience, and the creation of a suitable mix of peers.

A related aspect is the size of the peer group. The norm seems to be in the range from four to ten, but larger groups are also to be found. Once again, this is influenced by the focus of the review and the expertise needed.

The common criteria applied in the *selection of peers* to suit the purposes of the review are outlined above. Other differences in practice concern who chooses the peers and how formal their appointments are (including the responsibilities that they are expected to fulfil). Here practice varies considerably. In some cases peers are selected by an administrator in the agency; sometimes peer groups themselves nominate members; in some cases the group being reviewed is able to comment on the membership of the external visiting team.

A linked issue to the selection of peers is whether they have been provided with any *training*. There is considerable variation in this respect. The French CNE, for example, believes that training would undermine the principle of peer review and turn the peers into professional evaluators (Brennan *et al.*, 1994). There are, however, many forms of informal training or briefing of peers. These include a plenary meeting prior to the visit, participation of peers as 'observers' on panels before they are used as full participants, briefing documents (codes of practice, handbooks, regulations, etc), and seminars and workshops. The practice within the United Kingdom has been to give all peers formal training in the various agencies' assessment processes.

The main variation between agencies which undertake programme level reviews is whether a single team of peers reviews the subject in all the institutions or whether different teams are put together for each visit. The former is not easy to achieve in systems of higher education with a large number and diverse range of institutions, but it does provide a strong base for comparability between provision in different institutions and it also means that the overall process is probably fairer. The growing diversity of higher education systems, however, implies that separate review teams need to be set up to match the mission and goals of the group being reviewed.

Issues of selection, training and types of peer reflect differences in emphasis and in values. Where an agency has its own explicit values and criteria of quality, it will need to ensure that these are implemented in the assessment process and not substituted by shared disciplinary values of the assessors and assessed. To pre-empt this possibility, agencies will need to control selection, provide strict guidelines for the assessment process and train peer groups in their use. Otherwise, there will be a strong tendency for the visiting peer group to 'go native'.

Site visits by external peers involve the review of relevant documents (in particular the self-evaluation report and any supporting documents provided by the group being reviewed) and face-to-face discussions with appropriate people. Face-to-face discussions are a common feature of teaching evaluation but are not generally used in the evaluation of research. Classroom observation is rarely used as a method of peer evaluation although it has been a central feature of UK practice in recent years. There are differences in the range of people with whom discussions are held. Depending on the focus of the review, most involve relevant institutional staff (managers, administrators, teaching staff). In many cases students are also involved.

The length of review visits varies from one to four days, depending partly on whether classroom observation is required and partly on the nature of what is being reviewed (organization, curriculum, etc). Visits also vary in terms of whether they are standardized to meet specific agency guidelines and requirements, whether they are determined by the peer review team, or negotiated in advance of the visit with the group being reviewed.

A published report

The final element of the general model is the publication of a report. Most national agencies produce written reports of individual evaluations which are public documents and are made available to the higher education system as a whole and to other relevant stakeholders. Because public reports are written for dissemination to a wide group of people, there is a tendency for them to be bland and general in their content. Sometimes a private report is provided for the group being reviewed or for management in the institution; these reports are usually designed to provide a more critical analysis and to address the more sensitive issues. In Denmark, however, all the documentation produced for an evaluation is available to the public (including the self-evaluation reports).

There are two main types of report that emerge from the quality assessment process. One is the report of a particular institutional review or programme/subject review and the other is a national report bringing together information about developments in a given subject area across all universities in the country. Some agencies (for example, the UK funding councils) produce both types of report. The Danish Evaluation Agency produces only system-wide reports. These may contain relatively little information about an individual institution.

Differences in reporting relate to the summative and formative purposes of external assessment. Where the former predominate, reports need to contain explicit – often quantifiable – statements of outcomes. When the assessment is linked to an accreditation-type decision, the outcome is expressed in a pass–fail form. Where the purpose is to provide market information, the outcomes of assessment may take the form of a point on a numerical scale. Summative assessments lend themselves to rankings and to the construction of 'league tables' of institutions. Where the emphasis is formative, there will be greater emphasis placed on recommendations and the report will be written more directly for an academic audience. As we shall see in later chapters, the form of reporting of the results of quality assessment has a strong influence on the type of impact it makes.

A linked issue is who follows up the recommendations made in the evaluation reports. In general it appears that individual higher education institutions are held responsible to act on them. In some countries the ministry of education has formal responsibility for follow-up. In the Netherlands, for example, the Inspectorate for Higher Education from the Ministry for Education visits all higher education institutions two years after the publication of the external review report. The inspectors check on the measures that have been taken on the recommendations made by the visiting team. In Germany (Lower Saxony), where the external quality assessment system is a recent development (the agency was set up in 1995), the department that was reviewed has to prepare, three months after the peer review visit, a list of measures which will be taken to act on the recommendations. Two years after this, the department has to present an interim report setting out the changes that have been made to date.

We have used the general model to describe the many variations which exist in the methods used by national quality agencies. The variations are considerable. In part, they reflect differences in purpose and in national context. Purposes reflect, among other things, the extent to which quality assessment is being used by the state as a method of control and accountability. While such features are always there to some extent, they may be less important in systems where the state possesses many other forms of control and regulation over higher education, as is generally the case in continental Europe. An important feature of national context is system size. There are obvious difficulties in getting peer review systems to work effectively in small countries. And in large countries, peer review faces problems of scale and diversity. Thus, the elements of the EU's general model seem to apply most easily to medium-sized countries in continental Europe. Outside continental Europe, assessment systems tend to be more pluralistic, both in terms of the range of agencies in existence and in terms of the methods used. In the following section, we consider in more detail two examples of quality systems which approximate to the general model and an example of a system with rather different elements.

One model or many?

The first example is of the Dutch VSNU system, which appears to fit very well into the general model and has been influential in other European countries (for example, the systems in Lower Saxony in Germany and in Flanders in Belgium are based on the Dutch model). The second example is of the Centre for Quality Assurance and Evaluation of Higher Education in Denmark, which provides some unique additional features to the general model. Both these examples are of small to medium-sized higher education systems and yet contain important differences in approach to quality assessment. The third example is of evaluation systems in Mexican higher education and provides a contrast to the first two. The Mexican system is complex and consists of several forms of evaluation by different national agencies and at different levels in a very large higher education system. As noted in Chapter 4, the higher education institutions in Mexico were in financial crisis during the 1980s and the introduction of quality assessment there was very closely associated with funding issues.

Quality assessment in the Netherlands

The Association of Dutch Universities (VSNU) undertakes quality assessment of universities in the Netherlands. The system of quality assessment used by the

VSNU was set up in the mid-1980s following a recommendation in a Ministry of Education policy paper – *Higher Education: Autonomy and Quality (HOAK)*. This policy paper had initially suggested that universities be subjected to evaluation by an inspectorate but universities resisted this; the VSNU system was developed as a result. The Dutch system of higher education, as in other countries in Europe, was undergoing many changes and the new policy on assessment was developed to allow more autonomy and to encourage decentralization of the management of higher education institutions. The system of quality assessment was, on the whole, introduced so that institutions could prove that they were providing education of high quality in the context of their greater autonomy. It was also intended to support improvement within Dutch universities. It should be noted, however, that in international terms, the Dutch higher education system remains relatively highly regulated.

The VSNU is a private organization which is financed and governed by the 14 Dutch universities. 'It is both an association with external representative purposes as well as a service organization that provides services for the universities themselves. It can be regarded as the universities' branch organization' (Zijderveld, 1997: 2). The organization and management of external quality assessment of both education and research is one of these services. Others include providing courses and seminars, serving as a platform for inter-university deliberations, and acting as a representative of the universities in negotiations with central government.

The VSNU undertakes assessments at the programme level. They are designed to fulfil three main goals: quality improvement, accountability to society at large, and self-governance of higher education institutions. The system is intended to complement internal processes of quality assurance in universities. Programmes are assessed discipline by discipline on a six-year cycle on a nationwide level. Universities pay for the assessments themselves and, with the VSNU, are responsible for the organization and design of the system. There is no direct link between the outcomes of the quality assessments and the funding of programmes.

The assessment starts with a *self-analysis* which is the cornerstone of the system and which is intended to outline the strengths and weaknesses of the programme. The emphasis is on the contents and academic level of the programme. Organizational matters which are not directly relevant to the quality of the educational provision are not taken into account. The VSNU guidelines specify that the following issues should be covered in the self-analysis: the basic philosophy and intended level of achievement, the contents, masters theses (a cross-section of these are reviewed by the external peer review team), number of students and completion rates, barriers to the smooth running of the programme, facilities and infrastructure, graduates, staff, international elements of the programme, and internal system of quality assurance.

Independent peers are chosen to make up a *review committee*. The committee usually consists of four experts from within the discipline itself. Care is taken to ensure the impartiality of these members. In addition to the peers, there is one member with expertise in the education sciences plus a student member. The

VSNU provides a secretary to assist the review committee. The same review committee visits all the programmes in the same discipline in all the universities.

Prior to the site visits to the institutions members of the review committee are provided with copies of all the self-analyses and a sample of masters' theses from each of the programmes. All members individually examine each of the self-analyses and complete a checklist of issues.

A few weeks before the first of the visits in a given discipline, the committee meets to discuss the frame of reference, the basic criteria that each of the programmes should meet, and the issues that should be addressed during each of the visits. Each visit usually lasts two days and the committee picks up on issues that were not answered in the self-analyses and aims to acheive a 'multidimensional' view of the programme. Discussions during the visit are held with the group that prepared the self-analysis, the committee responsible for educational matters and quality assurance processes, students, teachers, student-counsellors, graduate students, and the faculty board responsible for the management of the programme.

At the end of each visit the chairman of the review committee presents an oral report of the committee's preliminary conclusions. After a few weeks an interim report outlining the committee's conclusions and recommendations is sent to the faculty board for comment. Once the faculty board's comments are received the programme report is finalized.

After the last visit for a given discipline, the programme committee drafts the final report. The final report includes all the individual programme reports and a comparative analysis of all the programmes. The report is then made public.

To fulfil the two goals of improvement and accountability, the final report must give an indication to the institutions of the quality of their educational programme and how this can be enhanced, and must also provide an insight for the general public into the quality of the different educational programmes in the discipline.

Copies of the final report are sent to each faculty board and university management and to the Inspectorate of Higher Education. These are the key people involved in the follow-up of the assessment who are called upon to address the quality improvement aspect. In addition, reports are circulated for accountability purposes to a number of other organizations, including the Ministry of Education, the Royal Dutch Academy of Arts and Sciences, employer organizations, government advisory councils on education and research, student unions, university newspapers and national newspapers.

The Inspectorate of Higher Education, which reports directly to the Minister of Education, is responsible for the overall follow-up and monitoring of the external reviews and for the assessment of the quality assessment system as a whole. If the inspectorate finds that the measures being taken in an institution to address the recommendations made by the VSNU review committee are inadequate, then the Minister of Education is informed. A possible consequence of this is a further analysis of the programme in an institution by the inspectorate itself. The ultimate conclusion of such an analysis by the inspectorate could be the striking off of the programme from the register of recognized (i.e. funded) programmes. This has never happened. The Inspectorate has followed up on a very small number of programmes in the universities and all these further investigations have resulted in satisfactory outcomes.

A similar system operates in the Dutch 'polytechnic' sector where the co-ordinating body is the institutions' representative body: the Association of Dutch Polytechnics and Colleges.

The Dutch experience most closely accords with the elements of the general model, which is not so surprising in view of its influence in shaping it. It also offers a good example of a national system in which disciplinary values appear to predominate. This is not just because it operates at the programme level. The existence and functions of the subject committees ensure that the assessment process is tailored to take account of disciplinary characteristics. Visits are chaired by subject experts. The visit focus is on academic content. The agency – in this case the VSNU – sets a framework for the quality assessment process, but it does not attempt to define what quality is, nor to set criteria for visiting groups to follow irrespective of discipline. There is also a clear division between assessment and decision-making functions, with the former the responsibility of the subject committees and the latter the responsibility of the universities and the ministry, with the Inspectorate occupying an intermediate advisory and policing function.

Quality assessment in Denmark

Two factors resulted in the introduction of external quality assessment in Denmark: rapid growth and state deregulation. Quality assessment in Denmark is also at the programme level and is carried out by the Centre for Quality Assurance and Evaluation. This Centre was established in 1992 by the Danish parliament with the support of the Committee of Chairmen of the National Educational Councils. There are five such councils in total, each representing one of the major subject areas (humanities, technical, health, natural sciences and social sciences). They are advisory bodies and the Minister of Education appoints their members. Most members are from the institutions of higher education and, in effect, the councils act as buffers between the ministry and the institutions (Rasmussen, 1997).

The Centre sees itself as an independent institution although funded by the Ministry of Education. The Centre formally undertakes evaluations at the request of either the ministry or the educational councils. Institutions are obliged to participate. Evaluations are of teaching only and have three main purposes:

- accountability to the Ministry that institutions are performing their deregulation responsibilities in an appropriate manner;
- to support decision-making in institutions;
- to provide higher education's markets with public information (Thune, 1997).

Thus, the main audiences for quality assessment are the government, the institutions themselves and the clients/customers. An added dimension to all evaluations is international comparability. All programmes are evaluated on a regular and systematic basis every five to seven years.

The evaluations are based on a standardized procedure which entails the following main elements: a steering committee, a self-assessment report, a user survey, a site visit, a conference, a report and a subsequent follow-up.

A *steering committee* is established for each programme evaluation to review the teaching of a particular subject across all of Denmark's higher education. The quality and integrity of each of the members is regarded as very important. Members are academics from the subject area of the evaluation and must be independent of the study programmes under review. The members of the steering committee are usually from Denmark and the other Nordic countries (not only because of the language advantages but because they usually have a basic knowledge of the Danish educational system). There are typically between four and six members in all and, as a general rule, one or two of the members will be employers of the graduates from the study programme being evaluated. The steering committee is charged with the professional responsibility for the evaluation and for the analyses, conclusions and recommendations in the final evaluative report.

Each institution prepares a *self-assessment report*. Institutions are asked to set up a self-assessment team with responsibility for drawing up the report. The Centre's staff organize meetings to help institutions prepare good quality reports. The Centre requires comparable self-assessments from the various institutions involved in an evaluation of a given programme and, therefore, provides guidelines on the themes that should be covered. These include the following: overall aims of the study programme; general aspects of the institution; disciplinary environment; study programme; relevant study and programme conditions; postgraduate and PhD programme; co-operation and interaction of the discipline with other research and educational institutions in Denmark and abroad; social structure of the student body. The report is expected to identify and discuss the central aspects of the study programme as well as its strengths and weaknesses in relation to its objectives. The report should also set out proposals for improvements to the study programmes under review.

All study programmes have external examiners who submit annual reports to the institutions. These reports contain examiners' appraisals and criticisms of the quality of the programme. Institutions are asked to include a summary of the *external examiners' reports* in their self-assessment report.

In addition to the documentation arising from the self-assessments, the Evaluation Centre undertakes *user surveys* of students, of recent graduates and of employers. The surveys present an assessment of the quality of the study programmes, as well as their strengths and weaknesses, from the perspective of the users. The Evaluation Centre, in consultation with the steering committee, identifies the themes to be covered. External consultants are commissioned to carry out the surveys.

Site visits are made to all the study programmes being evaluated. The steering committee, sometimes supplemented by other experts, acts as the visiting team. The visits are usually a day long and discussions during it are based on the

the infrastructure and improve the quality of services of higher education institutions. The fund provides resources for implementing activities identified by the institutions through their evaluation and planning processes. A key element of the fund is follow-up by random observation visits from expert examiners. These visits have shown that the fund has not only significantly helped to improve the facilities and physical conditions of institutions but has also helped to modernize their views of governance, administration and academic development (Valenti and Varela, 1998).

In addition, there are arrangements for the assessment of *individuals* which specifically focus on the achievement and productivity of academic staff. This is co-ordinated by the National Council on Science and Technology (Consejo Nacional de Ciencia y Tecnología – CONACYT). Committees formed by scientists undertake evaluation. Two main schemes are currently in operation.

In 1984, a National Researchers System was established which evaluates individual academics on their research productivity and gives additional tax-free income (i.e. on top of basic salary) on a monthly basis to researchers as a reward for the efficiency and quality of their work. Researchers who wish to participate in the scheme submit their curricula, publications and scientific papers. The applications are evaluated by peer groups on the basis of the quality, quantity, impact, originality and technical complexity of the research and technological development activities during a fixed period of time.

A National Programme for Teaching Careers was established in 1990 to evaluate and recognize good teaching. The criteria and methods for such an evaluation are developed by academic committees within each institution. The committees, which include prestigious staff members, evaluate the applications on criteria of quality, productivity and academic relevance. This programme also rewards individuals in the form of monthly bonuses (Valenti and Varela, 1998).

CONACYT also manages a National Register of Excellent Graduate Programmes, keeping track of graduate programmes which provide top quality student training. Students entering these programmes are given a scholarship by CONACYT in order to help them undertake their studies. Peer evaluation committees monitor both the entry of excellent programmes to the register and the award of student scholarships.

In addition to the institutional and individual evaluations outlined above, Mexico has in place evaluations of the achievement of students/alumni. A National Evaluation Centre (Centro Nacional de Evaluación – CENEVAL) was established in 1993 to develop and administer standardized examinations to test the knowledge and skills of students leaving secondary school as well as those finishing undergraduate (bachelor) degrees in specific fields (e.g. medicine, veterinary science, engineering, architecture, business). Participating in examinations at the former level is compulsory but the latter level is voluntary both for the institutions and the individuals.

The Mexican case reveals a range of assessment schemes administered by different agencies and operating at different levels. There are funding consequences arising from most of the assessment schemes. Mexican higher education is a large and complex system which enjoys considerable autonomy from government. In the absence of many of the regulatory mechanisms available to governments in continental Europe, assessment has a more summative emphasis and the link of assessment outcomes to financial rewards (at both institutional and individual levels) provides a form of market regulation to academic work.

Conclusion

Each national quality assessment system manifests its own particular pattern, responding to the features of the national higher education system and its relationships to government. Looking at the IMHE case studies as a whole we detect in the characteristics of the national quality systems an element of compensation for the dominant form of these existing relationships. Thus, assessment systems in the United Kingdom appear to take a more summative approach and to emphasize accountability in a system traditionally characterized by a high degree of institutional autonomy. A more formative approach and improvement orientation is found in continental Europe, where government control over higher education is clear and accepted. Governments are involved in the follow-up of assessment results in ways that would be unthinkable in other higher education systems. While quality assessment in the United Kingdom introduces more external control, quality assessment in continental Europe relaxes that control and, as we shall see in later chapters, helps support a greater degree of decision-making at institutional levels, albeit set in a firmly state-managed system.

Although we have followed the 'general model' of external quality assessment in structuring this chapter, we have noted considerable variations in how it is implemented in different countries. These reflect practical considerations to do with the size and diversity of the higher education system as well as political and sociological factors connected with the role of the state, the extent of consumerism and the traditions of institutional autonomy.

Whatever their formal ownership and funding, national quality agencies derive much of their legitimacy from the academic authority of their peer group committees and visiting panels. To an extent, therefore, they suggest a reinforcement of disciplinary academic values in the management of higher education. However, this would be too simplistic a conclusion. Depending on the level and focus of the assessment process, on the extent to which the agency stipulates clear criteria of quality and enforces them by guidelines and training of peer assessors, and on the extent of the inclusion of employers, students and educationalists in the conception of a peer group, a peer review evaluation process could in principle be used to transmit values other than those held by academic peers. Whether or not this is the case in practice will be the subject of later chapters on the impact of quality assessment.

6
The Methods of Quality Assessment in Institutions

Introduction

This chapter describes the variety of approaches to quality management and assessment adopted by the institutions which provided case studies for the IMHE project. The differences in approach are related to many factors, including changing institutional contexts and needs and the requirements of external quality agencies. These internal and external factors interact with each other to shape institutional approaches to quality management. With a growing requirement for higher education institutions to be accountable, the chapter shows how management of quality in institutions is becoming more centralized and regularized through the establishment of formal systems and procedures, the creation of quality committees and the assumption of management responsibility for quality matters by senior managers and administrators.

Long-standing concern for quality

Universities have existed as respected institutions in the eyes of society for a long time. Their governance, authority and status have however been increasingly questioned in the last two decades or so in many parts of the world. With the growth in the demand for higher education, the widening diversity in the range and type of institutions and courses, the changes in age and profile of the student body, and the growing pressures on available funding, there has been an increasing demand on higher education institutions to be accountable for all their activities. However, even before these changes, universities had well-established procedures through which quality and standards were maintained.

As Martin Trow questions,

> how did the great universities of the world come to be so productive of research and scholarship, of trained and educated people, and of wide

services to their societies over the past century and a half without much or any formal external assessment of their quality?

(Trow, 1994a: 7)

Trow goes on to suggest that, to a large extent, their scholarly standards were achieved through the

> trust that societies have placed in the academics, trust in their competence, in their intrinsic motivations to maintain the quality of their work and its products, and in the institutionalized arrangements the academy and its disciplines have created over the years for the control and maintenance of quality.

(Trow, 1994a: 8)

Traditionally, universities have emphasized self- and collegial-accountability and self-improvement. They have trusted their staff, relying on the professionalism of academics to ensure their quality and standing in society. Some of the ways in which they have done this, as described by Trow, are through the processes of recruitment of teachers, selection of students, peer review of research and scholarship, and periodic scrutiny of curriculum and teaching. The quality of teachers was ensured through rigorous recruitment, appointment and promotion policies. Admission policies were intended to ensure that only the best, most able students were selected for entry by the institution. Regular assessment and examination enabled close monitoring of the performance and progress of individual students. Departmental and individual quality was judged on the basis of research and scholarly activity over a long timespan. In the past, these judgements have mainly been based on a peer review process and have included success in gaining research grants, publication and review in refereed academic journals. Reviews of the curriculum by departments and other basic units have ensured that the currency of the curriculum is maintained on an ongoing basis. More recently, the quality of teaching has commonly been ensured through student questionnaire evaluations and staff development activities specifically aimed at improving the performance of the teachers in the classroom.

These are some of the most commonly found ways in which institutions have maintained and enhanced quality. As can been seen, they incorporate procedures at all levels from the whole institution to individual staff. Of course, they were not all to be found in every institution, nor were they always applied in a consistent and effective way.

Reasons, levels and purposes of internal quality assessment

By long tradition, universities have demonstrated and maintained excellence in relatively informal and ad hoc ways. In small elite higher education systems, exclusiveness was generally sufficient to justify claims for quality to the rest of society. However, with the current changes facing higher education – massification, diversification and cuts in funding – has come pressure for institutions to be more formally accountable. These pressures have led to a growing emphasis on more explicit and systematic mechanisms for quality management and assessment within institutions.

Many of the case-study institutions had set up institution-wide quality assessment systems. In some cases, the *reasons* for their establishment stemmed from a need to respond to the creation of an external quality agency. But they also reflected broader processes of institutional change and new management needs. There were in addition several examples of departments or basic units which had initiated quality assessment activities for their own purposes. External quality assessment (or the threat of it) could provide an impetus for the creation of internal assessment processes which then became valued for their own sake by administrators and managers.

The *levels* at which institutional quality management is conducted can be the whole institution, part of an institution, an individual, or a combination of these. Quality management frequently involves processes of periodic internal review which are usually initiated and managed from the centre of the institution, but sometimes devolved to the basic unit for implementation with close follow-up and monitoring from the centre. The case studies suggest that the systems are becoming increasingly formalized and regularized, with continuous review being a strong element. In contrast to past traditions, institutional quality management is as much about accountability as it is about improvement and, therefore, emphasis is placed on regularized and systematic processes rather than one-off, ad hoc reviews for specific purposes. Figure 6.1 shows the levels and initiators of quality management which have been found in the case studies.

In the case studies, externally initiated quality activities usually involved some form of periodic review process. These were frequently initiated in response to the requirements of an external agency (self-evaluation prior to an external review) but other external factors, generally to do with legislative or funding

		Levels		
		Institution	*Basic unit*	*Individual*
Initiator	*External*	Legislation Funding QA Agency/review	Reviews	Research reviews Incentive schemes
	Internal	'Total evaluations' Data collection and analysis	Reviews Student surveys	Student admissions Staff promotions Staff appraisal Student surveys

Figure 6.1   Levels and initiators of quality management

requirements, could also indirectly lead to review and other quality management activity. Externally initiated quality assessment activity was generally at the basic unit or institutional level (not usually both). Internally initiated activities were at all levels, but practice differed in the extent of integration of levels.

The quality assessment systems seemed to be mainly concerned with issues of teaching, research, curriculum and student experiences, or with organizational matters, or a combination of both. They usually entailed collection of descriptive information (often statistical) and sometimes included evaluative elements. At the basic unit level, systems were usually concerned with academic and pedagogic values. Sometimes these were set within an institutional framework reflecting mission-related goals and values. At the institution level, values were related to institutional mission and processes of control and decision-making.

The *purposes* of internal quality assessment mirrored the two main purposes of external quality assessment, i.e. accountability and improvement. Accountability was not necessarily managerial: it could also reflect the exercise of collegial authority by an institution's central committees. Improvement could be related to seeking solutions to particular problems or comprise part of broader goals of institutional change and development. The case studies revealed a complex picture, with institutional quality management and assessment being closely linked to the establishment of systems and cultures of internal accountability. It was generally an aspect of a more general growth in authority at the central management level in the institutions.

In the examples which follow, the introduction of new forms of institutional assessment was variously associated with broader processes of institutional change or maintaining status and reputation, or as a direct response to requirements of an external agency, as part of the development process of a new national quality system, as a response to increased market competition, or as a means of providing new incentives for individual academic staff. Most were institution-wide initiatives.

The first example is of a university that developed a quality management system as part of its response to broader institutional changes. The University of Monash has recently grown to become the largest university in Australia through a series of mergers and amalgamations of smaller institutions. As a result it has a diverse range of cultures, courses, students and approaches to teaching and research (Baldwin, 1997). Although a national system of quality audit at institutional level was introduced at about the same time, the author argues that

the university had already recognized the need for more systematic development of its own procedures before the first quality audit in 1993. The series of amalgamations had only been finalized in July 1992. A lot of work had gone into developing procedures which would allow for the smooth integration of the new campuses into Monash structures. The academic leaders of the institution knew that the next stage involved attention to quality assurance mechanisms that would ensure a reasonable consistency across the university in its academic operations . . . there is no doubt that they were 'pushed along' by the national exercise.

(Baldwin, 1997: 283–4)

At Monash it appears that major institutional changes were the reasons for establishing institution-wide quality management. The introduction of national quality audit at institutional level helped the process but did not cause it.

The second set of examples reflected concerns about status and reputation in changing national and institutional contexts. Louis Pasteur University in France was concerned to maintain its strong international reputation as a leading research university. The university found value in linking internal quality management to external quality assessment. The latter was seen as providing valuable management information. In the case of Vantaa Polytechnic, effective quality management was seen as a key factor in achieving polytechnic status. For this institution, success in external assessment processes was vital to its long-term development as a significant higher education institution. Crucial government decisions would be based on its results.

In cases where a national quality agency was established and operational, it clearly influenced the development of internal systems. But it was seldom the only factor. In the case of the Cardiff University of Wales, for example, formalized and rigorous quality assessment processes had been established to meet contextual changes as well as the introduction of external quality agency requirements.

The third pair of examples reveals institutional quality assessment as part of the piloting of a new national system. In the early 1990s the Finnish Ministry of Education initiated its concept of institutional evaluation. The Universities of Jyväskylä and Oulu volunteered to participate in these evaluations on a pilot basis. The aim of the pilot evaluations was the assessment and development of all the activities of an institution and to develop a nationwide evaluation procedure which would be suitable for use in all Finnish higher education institutions. However,

the concept of quality was not defined or discussed in any detail, neither by the Ministry of Education or by university. In a rather vague way it was assumed that quality means anything and everything good.

(Liuhanen *et al.*, 1998: 5)

Although the evaluations were organized by senior management teams, the nature of the assessment processes differed between the two universities. At the University of Jyväskylä the emphasis was on the development of processes at the basic unit level while at the University of Oulu the emphasis was upon institutional decision-making.

Both institutions voluntarily undertook these one-off evaluations in anticipation of a national system of quality assessment. As a result of these specific initiatives, attention to quality in the institutions has become more focused and it seems likely that this will continue in the long term whatever the nature of the external quality system which has now been introduced. At the University of Jyväskylä it was described as the 'emergence of an evaluative culture'

(Välimaa *et al.*, 1998: 31). At the University of Oulu, the case-study authors describe how a one-off, ad hoc institutional evaluation can result in long-term and regular quality management procedures being established. The authors report that the 'institution evaluation was a success and resulted in a system of continuous assessment of teaching and education at the departments' (Liuhanen *et al.*, 1998: 11). These included greater student participation in teaching and planning, development of teaching methods and changes in curricula. It made the institution aware that 'change was going on and that it had to continue' (p. 11).

The fourth example concerns initiatives taken at faculty level to help secure success in an increasingly competitive market for students. In common with the rest of the institution, the Open University Business School is subject to various forms of national quality assessment and to the quality assessment procedures set up by the university. However, the Business School chose also to participate in other external evaluations. The reasons for this were to do with the need to demonstrate the national and international standing of its programmes in a competitive context. The Business School opted for

> a range of quality assessment initiatives and systems primarily initiated and administered from outside the School . . . This reflects the School's position as a self-financing unit within a highly competitive educational market where external evidence of quality assurance and improvement are essential for survival and growth.
>
> (Brennan *et al.*, 1998: 10)

In addition to participation in the two main national quality assessment systems (then known as institutional audit and teaching quality assessment), the Open University Business School opted to subscribe to the following two externally led initiatives.

1. The Investors in People Standard. This is a UK-wide accreditation scheme aimed at establishing best practice in human resource management. To attain this standard organizations have to present evidence on 'policies, structures and practices pertaining to staff development (commitment to it, resources, management of it, links between staff development and business objectives, and evaluation of development at individual and organization-wide levels)' (Brennan *et al.*, 1998: 20).
2. Accreditation of the School's MBA programme by the Association of MBAs. This was an important recognition for the School which was useful for marketing purposes.

Both forms of external assessment gave the school valuable certification which it could use in the promotion and marketing of its courses.

The fifth and final example of institutional approaches to quality assessment is one which focuses at the individual level and appears to have as its principal goal the influencing of the priorities of academic staff through salary-linked incentive schemes. Individual staff members have not generally been the focus of external quality assessment systems. An exception is found in the case studies of the two Mexican universities – the Autonomous National University of Mexico (Universidad Nacional Autónoma de Mexico – UNAM) and the Autonomous Metropolitan University, Mexico City (Universidad Autónoma Metropolitana – UAM). A description of the national quality assessment system in Mexico which puts a great emphasis on the individual level is outlined in Chapter 5. And in Chapter 4 we have outlined the reasons for the introduction of individual level assessment in UAM. At both universities, the external and internal quality assessments are strongly linked to reward structures (both financial and reputational).

Within universities, traditional approaches to quality have focused on individuals (Trow, 1994a), for example through appointments and promotions procedures and the refereeing of research. Recent developments in quality management in some institutions are putting an increasing emphasis on the individual level, through staff development, appraisals and training. However, the main emphasis of new approaches is on collective activities to support quality, whether at institutional, faculty or departmental and programme levels. In the following section, we describe some of these approaches in more detail, drawing on the case-study institutions for examples.

Methods of quality assessment

Alongside traditional practices, often informal, through which the quality of academic work was maintained, formal procedures for quality management and assessment are being introduced in many institutions. These are generally managed from the centre of the institution, with new committees set up to oversee their implementation. New management posts are being specially created or existing staff portfolios changed to include formal responsibility for quality matters. The new procedures make such responsibility more explicit within institutions; they involve the systematic collection and analysis of information about the institution; and they frequently involve the introduction of some form of regular internal review. The examples we have selected emphasize the latter because it appears to be the most widespread new development. However, references are also made in some case studies to a wider set of procedures which together form an institutional quality system.

The first set of examples concern the institution-wide processes of internal review, of surveys and monitoring, of preparation and follow-up for external review, of the integration of internal and external review, and of multiple assessments for multiple purposes. These are followed by two examples of institutional quality assessment processes initiated at faculty level.

Institution-wide processes of internal review

The case study of Cardiff University of Wales provides a good example of how changing institutional contexts and the introduction of external quality assessment resulted in the introduction of a system of regular review. As noted in Chapter 4, Cardiff is one of the United Kingdom's largest universities and has a strong international reputation. Formed from the merger of two colleges of the university in 1988, it is the largest constituent institution of the Federal University of Wales.

New forms of quality assessment procedures started to be developed in the University after the merger. As an 'old' university in the UK system, Cardiff had not been subject to external quality assessment until 1992, when new legislation introduced institutional quality audit and programme quality assessment across all institutions of higher education in the United Kingdom. This was clearly an important factor behind Cardiff's decision to set up a formalized quality assessment system. Other factors which influenced the university were an increase in student numbers, the introduction of modularization and raised expectations of students, all of which put pressure on existing structures and practices.

The university has developed what it calls an Academic Quality System. This is based on (1) the corporate plan which sets out the university's mission and objectives; and (2) the quality policy which identifies the personal responsibility of staff to contribute to the provision of the students' educational experience within 'a supportive environment'. The system, developed in 1993, applies to all academic departments. Its purpose is stated as quality enhancement (the process of continuous improvement). It encompasses what the author of the case study sees as the two main internal institutional responsibilities (quality control and quality assurance)[1] and the externally imposed systems of quality audit and assessment which are regarded as a shared responsibility between the university and the national agencies (Daniels, 1998). Responsibility for the system lies with the Academic Quality Assurance Committee (AQAC) but a number of other relevant senior committees are also involved (the senate, research committee, teaching and learning committee, graduate research board, departmental boards).

The university has developed a comprehensive manual of the system which describes the internal quality assurance methods and incorporates 'feedback loops' (Daniels, 1998: 8) for the improvement of the education provision. The system involves an internal quality review process which the author of the case study describes as 'specific to the university . . . and not imposed by external requirements but influenced by them' (Daniels, 1998: 10). The methods include departmental self-review and peer assessment and are designed to

> evaluate the quality and fitness for stated purpose of the academic provision and the total student learning environment; evaluate the effectiveness of the department's quality assurance mechanisms; assist the department in its preparation for quality assessment; assess the department's research performance.
>
> (Daniels, 1998: 10)

Departments are selected for review on a rolling cycle of no more than five years (account is taken of the visits by external bodies to the departments to try to avoid duplication). Once a department has been selected for review by

AQAC, a departmental quality review team comprising the head of department and at least one other member of the academic staff is appointed, and a quality review panel including external advisers is appointed by the vice-chancellor. The department produces a departmental profile which

> describes and evaluates the quality of provision and research and which sets out how the department intends to achieve its targets for improving quality. Strengths and weaknesses, improvements to date and further antic-ipated improvements are included. Explicit criteria against which the department is making its judgements are identified.
>
> (Daniels, 1998: 10)

Before visiting the department the quality review panel receives the depart-mental profile together with other information such as degree scheme docu-mentation and schedules of assessment. The panel visits the department for between one and three days, produces a management report which contains an evaluation of the department's strengths and weaknesses, together with an assessment of its objectives and the extent to which they are being met; it places the work of the department in the context of the university's activities as a whole. The panel makes recommendations on any actions which need to be taken by the department. Implementation of the recommendations is monitored by AQAC. The department comments on the report and is asked to provide progress reports on the implementation of improvements. After the review one of the members of the panel is designated to maintain contact with the depart-ment in respect of quality-related matters. A year later this person meets with the head of department and senior colleagues before advising the relevant com-mittees on the progress made. The quality loop is completed at this stage.

The introduction of the internal quality review system is only one part of the changes in quality management that have occurred in Cardiff. In addition, the university has made many organizational and administrative changes at various levels within the institution to address quality management issues. For example, it has set up new committees or changed the remit of existing committees to include responsibilities for quality management, created new posts with respon-sibility for quality matters, changed the roles of heads of department to include responsibility for quality issues, and created staff development policies to pro-mote teaching development.

Institution-wide surveys and monitoring

As one of the leading research universities in France, the research output of the Louis Pasteur University in Strasbourg has traditionally been evaluated on an ongoing basis through, for example, publications, research contracts and prizes. However, the university decided that its other activities should also be assessed.

> The access to the university of a large and highly diverse public with very different expectations of what they stand to gain from a university

education has created new requirements for teachers . . . it remains difficult to assess how effectively teachers have responded to this demand . . . even though significant progress has been made in making non-research activities more crucial to the career development of teacher-researchers. Consequently, assessments and stock-taking of the education provided in universities and monitoring of student progress . . . have increasingly become a priority for the supervisory authorities . . . as elements of individual or collective evaluations . . . for institutions where assessment is aimed at improving the quality of teaching and providing criteria for teachers' career development; for student information . . . and as an indicator of a university's performance with respect to the mobility of its students and graduates.

It was in this perspective that the university undertook to develop its assessment tools in keeping with a growing worldwide trend.

(Cheminat and Hoffert, 1998: 7)

The university uses the following methods to achieve these requirements.

Student questionnaire surveys: Questionnaires to evaluate individual courses were developed in 1990. The questionnaires are anonymous and the results of the surveys are used as a tool for evaluation and dialogue with students. Teachers are free to use them at their discretion. The university has deemed it inappropriate to impose the surveys on a compulsory basis because it would have been difficult to get the teachers to accept the results as a relevant factor in their career development. The university has also, therefore, developed a more comprehensive questionnaire for evaluation of all course work leading to a diploma. This questionnaire aims to obtain

> quantitative information on how students perceive the education and training they receive and on the setting in which it takes place. This approach tends to encourage pedagogical dialogue among teachers and to provide information on which those responsible for training can base the steps taken to improve the quality of teaching and the conditions in which students learn.

(Cheminat and Hoffert, 1998: 8)

Monitoring internal cohorts: The university has developed software which enables it to evaluate over a seven-year period the time taken to obtain a diploma, the drop-out rates, and the number of students transferring to different programmes. The results make it possible to assess the impact on completion rates of new organizational or pedagogical measures.

Graduate employment: The university follows up the employment profile of its graduates through questionnaire surveys. The results from such surveys are presented to the University Council and disseminated widely to provide information for prospective students and other relevant bodies.

Evaluation and monitoring system: The university has a system in place that enables it to regularly monitor developments in its activities and management. For example, data collected on staffing ratios by discipline and by diploma and on the distribution of additional pay by category of staff, provide a valuable tool in teacher recruitment policy and for the monitoring of job applications submitted to the senior management of the university by individual departments.

As a prestigious research university where the academic credibility of staff is high, Louis Pasteur University has been concerned to develop procedures which do not undermine their professionalism. Therefore, the quality management system has an improvement rather than accountability orientation and the approach is collegial rather than managerial.

Institutional preparation for and follow-up of external review

The case study of Sheffield Hallam University in the United Kingdom provides an example of well-developed internal systems being altered in response to new external requirements.

Sheffield Hallam is a former polytechnic with long experience of external quality assessment under the aegis of the former Council for National Academic Awards. It therefore has an extensive and well-established framework for internal quality assessment. This is managed from the centre through the academic board and serves to achieve standard-setting, validation and evaluation, covering both teaching and research. The main elements of the framework include (1) annual quality review at course, unit, faculty and university levels; and (2) validation of proposals for curriculum changes and new courses.

In addition, since it became a 'new' university in 1992, it has developed an internal, institution-wide approach to the preparation and follow-up of external quality assessment at subject level. Responsibility for this rests with the Academic Quality and Standards Committee (AQSC) with input from a support team comprising assistant deans and subject co-ordinators. The process operates as follows:

A co-ordinator is identified by the relevant director of school for each unit of assessment to take responsibility for co-ordinating preparations for the quality assessment exercise. He or she then works with the support team to identify the range of evaluative and preparatory activities considered to be necessary for the subject area.

Whilst the subject group and the school are working through their action agenda, the draft self-assessment is also being prepared. This is scrutinized by the associated deans and senior registry staff and constructive advice given. The director of school is responsible for approving the final version for submission to [the external agency].

Arrangements for the visit are undertaken collaboratively by central and school-based staff. Formal communication with the university is via the academic registry.

Following the visit, all . . . reports are considered by school boards and by AQSC, with comments from school. AQSC highlights any notable issues for attention by Academic Board and other schools as appropriate.

(Arnold, 1998: 9–10)

In this way, external assessment is drawn into the institution's quality management processes. Institution-wide support services assist departments in preparing for – and doing well in – external assessments, and the institution ensures that follow-up action on the results of external assessment is taken at appropriate levels.

Internal and external review organized by an institution

The University of Newcastle in Australia provides an example of approaches to quality management at both basic unit and individual levels which has been initiated, tightly controlled and monitored by the head of the institution.

The university was established in 1965 and currently ranks among the top ten Australian research universities. A new vice-chancellor was appointed in 1993 at the same time as the Australian government introduced external quality assessment. The new vice-chancellor initiated reviews of most aspects of the university, and has taken overall responsibility for the quality process. The methods used involve the following main elements:

Internal self-review: A faculty self-review forms an initial and integral part of the strategic planning process and the university-organized external review of faculties. The aim of the self-review is

> to enhance the quality of the university's activities through each faculty's clarification of objectives, establishment of priorities, assessment of curriculum and pedagogical policies, assessment of research programs and examination of allocation of resources . . .
>
> The faculty self-review reports detail the goals of the individual faculties, consider the question of how well these goals are being met, document plans to remedy any deficiencies, and plans for further development . . . As part of the self-review exercise, all faculties and the two major administrative divisions produce a faculty strategic plan which contributes structurally to and cascades from the overall institutional strategic plan for the university.
> (Lester, 1998: 4–5)

The reports anticipate the external reviews which are organized by the Committee for University Development and Assessment (CUDA). This committee was established by, and reports to, the vice-chancellor. The committee develops terms of reference for the external reviews in consultation with the deans.

External review: CUDA guides the external review process by drawing up terms of reference, receiving reports from external reviewers, commenting on the reports, referring the reports and comments to the relevant faculty or administrative division and to senate, and advising the vice-chancellor on progress with implementation of the reviewers' reports over a period of time. Such reviews are at departmental level and take place on an 'as needed' basis.

Course review: This is undertaken by faculty boards on a five-year cycle. Reports of these are made to the academic senate. The reviews cover issues such as workloads, resources, facilities, and student and employer satisfaction.

A five-year teaching and learning development strategy: Such a strategy is designed to improve the quality of curriculum and teaching, and links up with a five-year budget strategy. It is implemented by a committee which reports directly to the vice-chancellor. Faculties are asked to justify the need for every subject recommended for continued inclusion in the university's curriculum.

External examiners: Examiners from overseas are appointed to mark research degree theses at both masters and PhD level. This is designed to ensure that the university's higher degrees are of international standard.

Staff appointment procedures: The vice-chancellor has the ultimate authority for the decision to fill posts at professor, associate professor and dean level. Deans are appraised every year: such appraisals can also be initiated at any time by the vice-chancellor. The appraisals are conducted by an 'independent facilitator' who makes a report to the deputy vice-chancellor. The deputy vice-chancellor discusses the reports with the dean concerned and makes a report to the vice-chancellor. When a dean's term of office comes to an end, the appraisal is used to make a decision on the continuation of the appointment. For the appointment of professors and associate professors, the vice-chancellor appoints two distinguished external scholars to sit on the selection committee.

Multiple assessments for multiple purposes

The variety and comprehensiveness of institutional quality management arrangements are described well in the case study of the Free University of Brussels. The case study provides a number of examples of quality management activities, some of which have existed for many decades while others are of more recent origin. These are the responsibility of various standing bodies in the university as well as of some temporary commissions.

The quality systems and processes described in the case study cover the recruitment and tenure of teaching staff, student appraisals of teaching performance, skill development of administrative and technical staff, selection and funding of research projects, and continuing and post-university training. The author of the case study describes not only the methods and criteria of assessment used in each case but also the follow-up actions taken as part of the quality management process. For example,

> Any member of the teaching staff who receives a negative [student] performance appraisal is strongly encouraged to meet students to discuss the grounds for the decision and to look for possible solutions. If this is the first negative appraisal received, the member of staff is invited to discuss the problem with the chairman of the teaching commission and one of its student members to look at the problems and envisage ways of remedying the situation.
>
> (Bodson, 1998: 33)

Repeated negative appraisals lead to escalating actions: a second negative appraisal results in 'a caution from the dean', a third and 'the case is submitted to the rector and the faculty council is informed' (p. 34). The author reports that improvements have generally followed such actions. Where they have not, although punitive actions are difficult to implement in the case of tenured staff, in the case of non-tenured staff 'there have been numerous cases in which staff with a series of negative appraisals have not applied for their contracts to be renewed . . . or have quite simply resigned' (p. 34).

As well as regular quality management activities at the university, the case study describes a number of special initiatives taken in order to tackle particular problems. One concerned under-achievement by first-year students. The case study describes the nature of the problem and the kinds of assistance provided to students in an attempt to remedy it (e.g. extra practice sessions, self-assessment sessions, drop-in guidance sessions, resource rooms, special seminars, guidance on use of the library). The effectiveness of these various kinds of assistance was assessed through student questionnaires and special 'before and after' testing of students.

This kind of three-step problem-solving process of quality management – problem identified, problem-solving measures introduced, impact of measures assessed – is of course quite common in universities, although one can also find examples where the third and even the second steps are not taken.

In 1994, the Free University of Brussels decided to undertake a special 'comprehensive assessment of quality' which was intended to involve the whole university community. There were both internal and external reasons for the assessment, the latter including the need 'to be prepared for possible outside assessments' but also reflecting the implications of recent legislation on university education and academic degrees and a desire to ensure transparency to outside bodies. A university-wide assessment was undertaken in three phases: (1) information collection and detailed analysis by each section/department, (2) general synthesis, initially by faculties, and (3) synthesis by the teaching commission.

> The documents resulting from this work will then provide a basis for a reorganization of programmes (in the broad sense) and for adjusting the workload of academic and scientific staff. They will also serve as a reference for developing a genuine faculty policy for staff and equipment resources. They will thus provide guidelines for both internal and external assessment, and the university may usefully draw on them in dealings with the public authorities on funding or indeed on statutory definitions of university curricula.
>
> (Bodson, 1998: 54)

The case study describes the assessment in some detail. It entailed an analysis of the objectives of each academic programme in terms of the skill profiles expected of graduates and the review of each constituent course in a programme in terms of its internal consistency, its consistency with other courses in its programme and, finally, the consistency between programmes. As a result of these activities (which had not been completed at the time the case study was being written) a number of academic programmes had been thoroughly reorganized.

The Brussels case study is a good example of multiple quality management activities being undertaken for multiple purposes, some internal and some external. Some of the activities were long-standing and part of regular university processes; others were special one-off activities responding to particular problems or circumstances.

Assessments at faculty level

Several of the case studies describe assessment activities undertaken in particular faculties and departments. As with institution-wide assessments, these were embarked on for a variety of reasons, some external and some internal to the faculty or department concerned. The University of Helsinki case study provides several examples of such assessment activities.

The Faculty of Science undertook self-assessment and international assessment of all its departments during 1993 and 1994.

> The self-assessment examined the state of the faculty, its strengths, obstacles to its effective functioning as well as measures which should be taken in order to improve the faculty's efficiency and to help it meet new scientific challenges and educational needs.
>
> (Hyvärinen *et al.*, 1998: 15)

The self-assessment process was followed by an international peer group assessment. The exercise as a whole led to many conclusions and recommendations, both about individual departments and the relationships between them. The case-study authors report that many of these recommendations have already been implemented.

Within the Faculty of Social Science, a self-assessment was undertaken in 1993 with the following objectives: to develop the strength and flexibility of degree contents and structures; to maintain a socially relevant degree structure; to ensure that the education both quantitatively and qualitatively answers labour market needs; and to develop a system of quality assessment appropriate for faculty practice.

A Faculty Teaching Development Committee was set up to oversee the assessment process. It did not attempt to impose a standardized assessment model on its departments. However, the case-study authors note that 'at many departments, systematic assessments remain a novelty or are still in their early stages' (Hyvärinen *et al.*, 1998: 22).

Assessment activities of a variety of sorts are described in other faculties at Helsinki. In the Economics Department, an assessment of departmental efficiency was undertaken.

> The Department wanted especially to assess personnel time management, since although nearly all the operating costs of the university's department are tied to personnel and teaching/work hours, they are nevertheless poorly known and understood . . . Data concerning personnel time

management was gathered in 1992–94. For follow-up and evaluation, a computer programme was created . . . The department's model for time management evaluation and follow-up and the publication of the assessment results attracted widespread interest within the university.

(Hyvärinen et al., 1998: 30)

At Helsinki, other such discipline-based assessments were conducted either out of the desire of the basic units concerned or as part of national and international assessment in the subject field. The assessments did not follow a standard university model nor reflect an overriding university purpose. Some university-wide assessment activities did take place but these were concerned with non-disciplinary themes such as international operations, regional co-operation, and university administration and management.

Several of the other case studies describe assessment activities undertaken at faculty or departmental levels. Such assessments may be carried out more or less independently of the parent university but can reflect issues and concerns of national and international networks in the subject field. An example is the assessment of engineering at the Autonomous National University of Mexico (Universidad Nacional Autónoma de Mexico – UNAM).

The School of Engineering at UNAM is a large, long-established school with a strong national and international reputation. The review and updating of study programmes is nothing new to the school. Curricula and academic organization reviews had taken place in 1944, 1958, 1967, 1979 and 1990. In 1979, committees for each major field of study were set up 'charged with the ongoing assessment of curricular content' (Rojo *et al.*, 1998: 26). In 1992, external advisory groups were established for the school's graduate divisions.

A new evaluation of the School of Engineering took place between 1993 and 1995. It was carried out in two stages; the first focusing on the role of basic sciences in the engineering curriculum and the second involving adjustments and specific changes for each engineering field.

The evaluation took place within a critical context of international competitiveness and global changes, and their effect or repercussion in the preparation of engineers; of a domestic and international review and development of educational accreditation and professional certification processes as a result of globalization; of an analysis of the development of the discipline and the technological innovations relevant in the field of engineering; and in the face of the many new problems facing society with impact on the different branches of engineering.

(Rojo et al., 1998: 26)

External inputs into the evaluation included the results of the Pan American Engineers' Association study conducted in 1991 on the appropriate contents of physics, mathematics and chemistry in the engineering curriculum; national evaluation guidelines prepared by the inter-institutional committees for the evaluation of higher education; and the implications of the North American Free Trade Agreement between Canada, Mexico and the United States which envisaged exchange of professional services, including engineering services (implying harmonization of accreditation and registration). The School of Engineering had also conducted a study of the career and professional development prospects and experiences of its graduates, the results of which were fed into the evaluation.

The school set up a special commission to undertake the review. The case study is a good example of how an internally generated assessment can have a strongly external orientation, sources of information and criteria of evaluation. It is also an example of how internal review can be critical and hard-hitting.

> In its first stage, the evaluation indicated the program to be outdated, lacking clarity regarding the objectives of the study plan, with content repetition, inadequate use of basic sciences, and an imbalance between core and peripheral topics.
>
> (Rojo *et al.*, 1998: 28)

The overall evaluation and programme renewal led to many changes.

> Besides the participation of different collegiate bodies at the school and institutional levels, it can be said that the whole school became involved in the process. The fundamental reference points in the evaluation sought to strike a balance between international considerations and benchmarks, and domestic and institutional conditioning factors, the criteria being always that of improving the professional quality of engineering graduates.
>
> (Rojo *et al.*, 1998: 29)

The review led to changes in academic governance, in curricula and in academic culture.

Conclusion

It is difficult to do justice in a single chapter to the wide range of methods of quality management and assessment described by the authors of the IMHE institutional case studies. Some have existed almost as long as the universities themselves, but many are of more recent origin, reflecting the changes taking place in higher education in the countries involved.

The majority of the quality management activities described in the case studies were initiated by the institutions themselves, rather than being forced upon the institutions by national quality agencies. However, changing external circumstances lay behind many new approaches to quality management. The approaches included the development of institution-wide systems, the introduction of regular reviews of subject provision and the widespread use of student surveys. New forms of accountability – to the state and to 'consumers' as well as to the academic community – called for new forms of quality management. In some institutions, these reflected the strengthening of institutional management processes more generally, of which more explicit lines of internal accountability were an important part. And in its turn, stronger institutional management was needed because of the greater complexity of the external environment and the need for faster decision-making to effect the changes perceived to be necessary to ensure future institutional success, and even survival.

If quality assessment appeared to be providing a useful management tool in many institutions, this did not necessarily imply that it was substituting management values for those of the discipline or wider academic community. Peer review remained the most important method of quality assessment, supported increasingly by surveys of students and graduates. But even when initiated internally, quality management and assessment activities frequently had recourse to external information and expertise, as well as reflecting external pressures and issues.

What then does this imply about the role of national quality agencies? Although most of the countries which participated in the IMHE study possessed such agencies, their activities were generally relegated to the background in the institutional case studies. In a number of the institutions, it was clear that the creation of an agency had provided a stimulus for the introduction of more formalized institution-wide quality systems. The existence of the agency and its requirements could also influence the timescale and focus of internal review. Although not in the forefront, the agencies were clearly not unimportant: but they were only one element in an increasingly wide spectrum of internal and external considerations influencing approaches to quality management within institutions.

We began this chapter by quoting Martin Trow to the effect that universities have had long-standing arrangements for ensuring the quality of their work. Our study suggests, however, that changing circumstances inside and outside institutions have required these long-standing arrangements to be augmented by newer ones. Quality management is increasingly formal rather than informal, explicit rather than implicit, managerially organized and controlled, more frequent and more comprehensive. It uses a multiplicity of methods for a multiplicity of purposes. It has become a central mechanism in the management of institutional change in higher education.

Note

1. The case-study author describes the meaning of these terms as follows: 'Quality control relates to the arrangements (procedures, standards, organization) within higher education institutions which verify that teaching and assessment are carried out in a satisfactory manner. Quality assurance encompasses all the policies, systems and processes directed to ensuring maintenance and enhancement of the quality of educational provision in higher education' (Daniels, 1998: 29).

7

Impact of Quality Assessment through Rewards

Introduction

As the last two chapters have made clear, quality management and assessment in higher education is a time-consuming process, whatever method is used. And for all of the reasons that were discussed in Chapters 3 and 4, staff in higher education institutions are under increasing pressure: pressures from more and different kinds of students, from new courses in new subject fields, from the expansion of knowledge, from the demands of new bureaucracies and so on. Time for additional activities is increasingly scarce.

Quality assessment is seldom an entirely voluntary activity for those who undertake it. Varying degrees of compulsion – from external agencies, from university management, from outside events – are usually present. Staff engage in quality assessment because they have to, whatever the enthusiasm and commitment they may bring to the tasks or acquire in the process of carrying them out. The question, therefore, of whether it is all worthwhile, whether the time and resources devoted to quality management and assessment could not be put to better use in other ways, is inevitably raised in most institutions which undertake these processes. Does quality assessment bring benefits which outweigh the costs involved? Does it make an impact and, if so, on what?

In the next three chapters, we look at the various kinds of impact deriving from the assessment of quality in higher education. One of the major difficulties in so doing is the problem of determining causality. In institutions where so much is changing, it is not easy to detect the independent effect of any one factor. Frequently we are told that changes made in response to quality assessment 'would have happened anyway'. And some of them undoubtedly would have.

In this chapter, we first look at some of the difficulties of conceptualizing the impact of quality assessment. We then consider the extent to which it can occur through rewards associated with the results of assessment.

Conceptualizing impact

In Chapter 2, we referred to four different levels of impact: system, institutional, basic unit and individual. To these different levels, we now need to add questions about mechanisms (*how* impact occurs), questions of timing (*when* impact occurs), questions of agency (*who* determines impact) and finally to make a distinction between *direct* and *indirect* forms of impact. We shall then use these distinctions to discuss *what* is the impact of quality assessment.

Questions of mechanism, timing and agency are all interconnected. We consider them separately below for conceptual purposes but, in reviewing the examples provided by the IMHE case studies, we will see how they relate to each other.

We shall refer to three mechanisms of impact in Chapters 7 to 9: impact through rewards; impact through changing policies and structures; and impact through changing higher education cultures. We will discuss these three mechanisms, together with some examples of them, later. Here, we want to indicate the relationship between impact and some of the aspects of assessment method discussed previously. Thus, impact through rewards is likely to be a function of the *published outcomes* of assessment, in particular the nature of any summative judgements (numerical or otherwise) and their effects on funding, reputation, influence and so on. Impact through changing policies and structures is likely to be in response to the overall pattern of the *internal quality assessment methodology* as institutions organize themselves to respond to the requirements of external assessment. But, in addition, the impact of policy and structural changes might arise in response to *recommendations* made in particular assessment reports, concerning either specific programmes/departments or the institution as a whole. Impacts through changing cultures are likely to arise from experiences of the *self-evaluation process* and the effects of *institutional quality assessment procedures*. The relationship between methods of assessment and mechanisms of impact is summarized in Figure 7.1.

In considering the *timescale of impact*, variations according to both mechanisms and method can be expected. Thus, cultural change is likely to be a slow process taking place over several years. Attitudes and behaviours relating to teaching and to relations with students are central to academic cultures and self-images,

	Mechanism of impact		
Method of assessment	*Rewards*	*Structure and policies*	*Cultures*
Self-evaluation			X
Institutional QA		X	X
External evaluation reports	X	X	

Figure 7.1 Methods of assessment and mechanisms of impact

are deep-rooted and unlikely to change quickly, if at all. Indeed, one of the case-study authors in the IMHE project suggested that fundamental cultural change would only be achieved with the socialization of a new generation of academics. Structural and policy change can, in principle, be achieved more quickly, although institutional decision-making procedures are typically slow and cumbersome. However, a critical external assessment can speed them up no end. The impact of quality assessment through rewards can be immediate if the rewards are financial but only gradual if they are reputational.

Quality assessment can make an impact on an institution even before it has been carried out. The awareness that it is going to happen can induce policy and procedural change in anticipation of the assessment. The preparation of a self-evaluation and the process of getting ready for an external assessment visit can be euphoric or traumatic or something in-between. Staff relations and individual and collective self-conceptions can be affected. Reports of assessment visits and the recommendations which they put forward can help set the agenda for long-term change in a department or institution, but they can also be totally ignored.

The *agency of impact* (i.e. who is responsible) connects with issues of level and mechanism. Thus, impact through rewards will be determined largely outside the institution – by governments, markets and the wider academic community – although institutional managements in some countries may opt to distribute financial rewards in accordance with assessment results. Impact through policies and structures are likely to be achieved through institutional management processes while cultural change is primarily a matter for basic units/departments and individual staff members. Figure 7.2 summarizes these relationships.

Several authors have drawn a distinction between direct and indirect forms of impact (e.g. Välimaa *et al.*, 1997; Maassen and Westerheijden, 1998). Changes made as a result of recommendations contained in an assessment report (external or internal) are examples of direct forms of impact, as are the financial or accreditation decisions which sometimes follow external assessments. Changes in cultures, in relations between staff (including the development of new management practices), are examples of indirect impacts. Impacts upon funding are

	Method	*Timescale*	*Actor*
Rewards	External QA reports	Financial – immediate Reputational – long term	External groups Institutional management
Structures, policies	Institutional QA External reports	Dependent on institutional decision-making	Institutional management
Cultures	Self-evaluation Institutional QA	Long term	Basic units Individual staff

Figure 7.2   How quality assessment makes an impact on institutions

usually indirect. Direct impacts on one part of an institution may also be indirect impacts on others. It is arguable that it is the indirect impacts of quality assessment which are the more fundamental and long lasting.

Impact through rewards

In their much quoted report for the European Union, van Vught and Westerheijden identified 'no direct link to funding' as a fifth element of their general model of quality assessment (the other four being a meta-level co-ordinating agency, self-evaluation, peer review, and published reports) (van Vught and Westerheijden, 1993). However, unlike the other elements, there seemed to be a strong prescriptiveness about the fifth element of the model. There are understandable reasons for this. Financial consequences of quality assessment bring rewards and punishments into the process. In so doing, it is maintained, they change its nature.

Martin Trow has drawn a sharp distinction between evaluations concerned with learning and evaluations concerned with persuading (Trow, 1996). It is apparent that evaluations or quality assessments which have financial consequences will be of the latter type. After all, who is going to be self-critical if there are financial penalties for doing so? So, instead of promoting learning and self-criticism, the assessment process comes to be about persuasion and public relations, perhaps even involving deception.

There do not have to be financial outcomes hanging on the results of an assessment for it to become a public relations exercise. Any potential outcome which has value to the people being assessed (whether by self or external assessment) will foster an attempt to manipulate the process in order to achieve the desired outcome.

A useful example comes from a study which we carried out in England in 1996 into the impact of the quality assessment system of the Higher Education Funding Council (Brennan, Frederiks and Shah, 1997). This system had been introduced in 1993 and comprised self-assessment followed by external assessment, the results of which were rated on a three-point scale (excellent, satisfactory and unsatisfactory). The assessment process was undertaken at a subject level and was meant to focus on the quality of teaching and learning. The project was intended to investigate the impact of this process on the first fifteen subjects which had undergone it.

The fact of the rating on a three-point scale concentrated attention on the result of the assessment. Although a report of around 3,000 words was written about each assessment, it was the rating which mattered to many of the people we interviewed. Yet only in the case of an 'unsatisfactory' rating were there financial consequences from the assessment, and then they were indirect. The real consequence of the rating was on reputation and self-image.

To many of the people we interviewed who had experienced these quality assessments, the rating achieved mattered a lot. And the pre-knowledge that there was to be a rating as an outcome of the process had for some people created much anxiety prior to and during the assessment. However, others we interviewed seemed to have been fairly relaxed about the whole exercise and relatively unconcerned about the outcome. What lay behind these different reactions?

A number of factors appear to have influenced this differential response to quality assessment in England. First, many of the institutions which took part in the research had substantial previous experience of similar types of assessment as carried out by an accreditation body, the Council for National Academic Awards. Although this body was defunct by the time of our research, its memory lived on in the organizational consciousness of the institutions which had been subject to its controls. Thus, external assessment was nothing new; staff believed (sometimes wrongly) that they knew what to expect and assessment had become something akin to a familiar ritual.

A second factor which influenced response was the approach taken to quality assessment by senior management in the institutions. Although relaxed in many cases, in some the institutional leaders showed a marked nervousness about the assessment exercises. In one case, this even involved the institutional head attending classes in a subject that was shortly to be assessed. More commonly, staff meetings were arranged – one faculty taking its entire academic staff to a country hotel for two days of assessment preparation. Whatever else preparations of this sort achieved, they certainly raised the stakes for the staff involved, emphasizing the importance that was attached to the assessment by the institution.

A third factor was the existing reputation of the institution or department being assessed. Quite simply, those with the highest reputations had more to lose from the assessment process. Where the collective self-concept was of 'excellence', an external judgement of anything less was viewed as failure. Where staff had no pretentions to 'excellence' in the first place, only the dire judgement of 'unsatisfactory' was likely to shock: and these latter judgements were very rare.

The responses to the English quality assessment system owed much to distinctive features of the assessment methodology, in particular the summative judgement on a three-point scale. This aspect of the methodology has since been changed, although numerical rating is still involved. Few other quality assessment systems entail this sort of quantifiable outcome. Yet, in the case of external assessment processes, rewards and punishments were never far from the surface in many of the IMHE case studies. As well as the potential for rewards and punishments through reputation, quality assessment could involve rewards and punishments through institutional or programme *status*, through *income*, and through *influence*. We shall discuss each in turn.

Rewards of formal status allocation

Quality assessment linked to accreditation is probably the most common example of how assessment can affect *status*. This has become the normal practice in the countries of central and eastern Europe, replacing the regulatory mechanisms of the former communist governments. In considering the rewards of quality assessment, it is always worth considering *who* is providing them. In the case of accreditation systems in these countries, the answer is unequivocally the state. Accreditation is a prerequisite both for state funding and for the recognition of degrees and diplomas (EC PHARE, 1998a). In contrast, accreditation in the United States brings rewards in the market place rather than formal government or state rewards (Dill, 1997).

Elsewhere in Europe, accreditation linked to quality assessment is not common. There are, however, other ways in which the results of quality assessment can lead to status rewards from the state. A common one is the award of an institutional designation, such as 'university', 'polytechnic', etc. This can be very important during periods of system restructuring as was happening in Finland during the IMHE project.

The case study of Vantaa Polytechnic in Finland can be best described, using the words of the authors, as 'Striving for a Licence'. A polytechnic system in Finland allows individual institutions to achieve permanent status as polytechnics following an initial experimental stage. At the time of the IMHE project, Vantaa was still in the experimental stage, having failed at an initial attempt to achieve the desired status in 1995. To obtain a permanent licence, an institution must 'fulfil an educational need and meet quality criteria for the provision of higher education' (Antikainen and Mattila, 1998: 7). As the case study notes, quality assessment in order to obtain the licence has been undertaken alongside other evaluation activities connected with the internal development of the institution: evaluation is described in the report as a 'cornerstone of the strategy and practice of Vantaa Polytechnic' (p. 28). Evaluation connected with the licensing is described in the report as a 'frustrating process' which has influenced negatively 'staff's and students' motivation to their work' (p. 29).

As is common with quality assessment linked to the award of an institutional status, formal criteria are specified. In the case of the Finnish polytechnics, there are 12 criteria with, according to the case-study authors, 'no specifications offered in legislation of what is meant by the criteria' (p. 7). The frustrations of the licensing process are further elaborated in the case-study report:

> the polytechnics vying for the permanent or experimental licence can apply annually until a set number of polytechnic institutions and polytechnic level openings are reached . . . The assessment process preceding the granting of the permanent licence has so far taken place twice, both times by grading forms filled out by the applying polytechnics. The form comprises a given set of questions following the formulations of the twelve quality criteria given in the Act.
>
> (Antikainen and Mattila, 1998: 7)

While this sort of assessment process is clearly understandable in terms of the needs of government to control institutional designations and recognition, it is not in its nature likely to generate internal change and improvement. The point is demonstrated at Vantaa by the large amount of assessment and evaluation which is undertaken without direct connection with the licensing process. Similar patterns may be occurring within the accreditation systems of central and eastern Europe (see the case studies of the Hungarian Bessenyei and Kolcsey Colleges and the final report of the PHARE project, EC PHARE, 1998b). What this suggests is that quality assessment activities linked to state rewards of formal status may not be compatible with other objectives of assessment, such as improvement and institutional change.

Assessment linked to accreditation and licensing is an extreme example of the status reward function of quality assessment. In these cases, it is in the forefront of the assessment activity, its primary raison d'être. But there are other cases where quality assessment can impact upon status. Thus, the Aalborg case study describes how the status of the university's history programmes came indirectly to be threatened as a result of the national evaluation process (Rasmussen, 1997). And in the Netherlands, although the evaluation processes are not undertaken by state bodies, the results of the evaluations can, via the Dutch Inspectorate for Schools, be used by the ministry to close down poor quality educational provision. However, it must also be emphasized that such powers are seldom used (a full history programme continues to exist at the University of Aalborg).

In cases where governments possess regulatory controls over higher education – and all do to some extent in respect of state provision – it is bound to be the case that the public results of external quality assessments may be taken into account in the exercise of such controls. Such cases are best described as indirect forms of impact upon status. They are not at the forefront of assessment activity. As the Dutch and other case studies show, there is no incompatibility between this sort of indirect status reward (punishment is perhaps a more appropriate phrase) and the improvement and change impacts of quality assessment. This will become clearer from some of the case studies to be discussed in Chapter 8.

Rewards of income

Examples of the direct impact of assessment on institutional income are very rare. They are more likely to occur indirectly as a consequence of status gain or removal (see above). Other forms of indirect financial impact are through markets (students, employers, research funders) which may themselves be influenced through the reputational gains and losses which can occur as a result of assessment. One or two countries (e.g. England) have initiated special competitions for the funding of educational development projects, with entrance to the competition being dependent on a good assessment result (HEFCE, 1997).

The linking of quality assessment to funding is problematic. There may be a desire to reward the 'successful', but this would involve the state paying more for an already good 'product'. Punishment of the 'unsuccessful' carries with it similar undesirable consequences. Education of low quality is unlikely to be improved by the reduction of funding. This dilemma is occasionally resolved by funding additional student places at the 'best' programmes or institutions, but this is usually only a real option in times of expansion of student numbers. Thus there is a general reluctance to link the results of quality assessment directly to funding. An improvement logic would suggest that an inverse relationship might be to give more to the least good. The reward logic points in the opposite direction. Several of the case-study reports note expectations from academic staff that success in assessment should be financially rewarded, but in almost all cases, these expectations were disappointed.

The important exception to the absence of an assessment-funding link was to be found in the two Mexican case studies. The Mexican context has been described in Chapter 4. Briefly, it was one where depressed staff salaries had been improved substantially by the introduction of performance-related pay based on the results of multiple forms of staff evaluation, and where institutional funding from the state was thought to be enhanced by the existence of strong internal evaluation systems within the universities. These provided high levels of accountability for funding received from the state in an otherwise highly autonomous system.

The case study of the Autonomous National University of Mexico (Universidad Nacional Autónoma de Mexico – UNAM) reports some impressive performance impacts arising from its internal evaluation procedures. Since the introduction of these voluntary performance incentive schemes in the early 1990s, increasing numbers of staff have participated in them.

> The use of economic stimuli has resulted in greater participation of academics, in the various institutional programs recently established, and in their having the necessary quality requirements. More than two thirds (68%) of the institution's full-time academic staff (8672) are currently being supported by the Rewards Program, while in 1990 only 55% received support. With the Incentives Program for Lecturers and out-time Personnel, 8893 academics are being supported, accounting for 46% of the corresponding group; in 1993 – the year when the program was put into practice – support was provided to only 39% of the whole group. Through the University Awards, the work of 111 university academics has been recognized, while in the same period, a total of 101 promising young professors have received the University Distinction for Young Academics.
>
> (Rojo *et al.*, 1998: 18)

The authors report significant increases in staff qualifications (a 10 per cent increase in the higher qualification categories) and more external recognition for the quality of research work. These improvements can also be seen in student performance measures, with the graduation rate increasing by 33 per cent and the numbers of students covering all course credits in the required time increasing by 25 per cent (Rojo *et al.*, 1998: 20).

Before assigning these impressive improvements solely to the effects of the staff rewards schemes introduced by the university, it should be noted that such schemes were part of broader evaluation systems in the university. These covered curricula and other academic matters as well as organizational structures and administrative issues. The overall strategy of the university is summarized by the case-study authors:

> The University decided . . . to motivate its academics through programs designed, formulated and explicitly initiated to expand their horizons, but according to a critical path design which at the same time led to the re-awakening and consolidation of academic concerns. Concrete measures were taken, all framed within the characteristic participatory style of decision-making at UNAM, to set the guidelines for the development of the institution, renovate its management policies and plan an ongoing and systematic evaluation of its members. Measures were taken along these lines for an administrative re-organization of the institution which would allow a more efficient use of resources, more expedient paperwork, the modification of job standards, the updating of curricula and study plans, the modernization of support facilities for academic endeavours, alternative sources of financing, and a change in the declining image that the University was experiencing.
>
> (Rojo *et al.*, 1998: 36)

The university was 'redefining its concept of quality' as part of a far-reaching process of the management of change. Reward systems for staff were an important part of this process, but they were only a part. Like other reward systems, they operated on largely quantifiable procedures mediated by institutional peer review processes. External quality systems (of which there are several in Mexico) are accorded little if any significance by the case-study authors in their discussion of the changes brought about by assessment. However, if external quality assessment systems seem to have been relatively unimportant in the case of UNAM, it should also be noted that external factors associated with funding – described in the case study as 'a crisis with serious consequences for academic life' (Rojo *et al.*, 1998: 36) – played a crucial part in stimulating the various assessment and management actions that appear to be transforming the university.

Similar personal incentive and reward schemes have been introduced in Mexico City's other main university, the Autonomous Metropolitan University (Universidad Autónoma Metropolitana – UAM). The case-study authors discuss the relationship between such institutional assessment and government assessment and funding policies. With regard to assessment policies, the university's strategy was essentially defensive. With regard to funding, it was largely competitive.

Various national assessment arrangements have been established within the traditionally autonomous Mexican higher education system. By introducing its own comprehensive internal quality system, UAM sought to limit the reach of external systems.

In the defensive sense, this position involved reaching a pragmatic agreement with the government allowing the university to take the quality
assessment mechanism into its own hands, thus avoiding the possibility that
some other mechanism that the university had not designed and did not
control would be imposed.

(Valenti and Varela, 1998: 7)

The competitive aspect was in respect of state funding. The authors suggest
that the establishment of an effective internal quality assessment system was,
in part, a strategy to help legitimize preferential government funding of the
university.

In this (competitive) sense, it is possible to think that one of the non-explicit
objectives of the official policy was to strengthen some specific institutions,
including the UAM, by means of financial mechanisms linked to quality
assessments . . .

(Valenti and Varela, 1998: 7)

The Mexican case studies are interesting from a number of viewpoints. First,
they are systems in which self-assessment by institutions predominates, notwith-
standing the existence of several national quality bodies. Second, they represent
quality systems which link directly to financial rewards for individuals. Third,
they have been largely accepted within the two universities under consideration
here. Staff interviewed as part of the UAM case study were broadly favourable,
although complex behavioural responses to the assessment schemes were also
hinted at.

The linkages between assessment, motivation, planning and funding are
emphasized by the authors:

quality assessment is shown as a useful instrument of educational policy,
because through this method a more dynamic and relevant mode of planning than had previously functioned has been established, penetrating all
levels of university operation. The ties between budget and goals, despite
the limitations of the arrangement, today permeate all aspects of university
life . . . There had not previously existed an important motivation for individuals to provide thorough information on their activities, because it had
no effect on their income or their daily tasks. Now the flow of information
is parallel to the operation of the system of fellowships and incentives, and
institutional quality assessment can be utilized as a university management
tool.

(Valenti and Varela, 1998: 30)

This last point is a useful reminder that even a largely descriptive self-assessment
system can have significant effects through the provision and influence of previously hidden information upon decision-making.

Rewards of influence

Power and influence – the capacity to impose one's will over others – can be altered by the results of quality assessment. Closely linked to their impact on reputation, favourable results of assessments at programme or departmental level can improve the standing and influence of the programme or department concerned within its home institution.

To do so, certain conditions must obtain. First, the assessment process should lead to an unambiguous (and preferably quantifiable) outcome. Second, that outcome should be a differentiating factor between the basic units of the institution, i.e. an 'excellent' outcome when others are 'average', or an 'average' outcome when the others are 'excellent' (the latter of course associated with loss of influence). Third, the outcome should be accorded legitimacy within the institution. Fourth, management and decision-making processes within the institution should be sufficiently centralized to permit action on the basis of the differentiating quality factor.

All four of these conditions pertained within the English Department of one of the universities we studied as part of a project investigating the impact of quality assessment in England (Brennan, Frederiks and Shah, 1997). The department existed in an unfashionable former polytechnic which had achieved university status only a few years before the study, and only two years before the assessment had taken place. In the words of the departmental head, the department had been politically weak within its institution. Its staff tended to be regarded as 'troublemakers', and its courses did not accord with the vocational and technological ethos which the university wished to promote.

As in all UK university departments, the English staff were assessed by external peers, separately in respect of their teaching and their research, as part of a national system of external assessment undertaken by the higher education funding councils. On both assessments, they received the highest possible ratings, implying that no other university was better in this subject field.

The immediate reaction in the department to the result of the assessments was described as 'euphoric'. And in the rest of the university, 'people stopped treating us like troublemakers and began to treat us like stars' (Brennan, Frederiks and Shah, 1997: 63). There was also a concrete financial reward, as the university decided to increase the department's funding by 10 per cent over two years. The department's standing within the university was transformed. In the words of one staff member, the rest of the university was now 'prejudiced to think we are good' (Brennan, Frederiks and Shah, 1997: 63).

In many ways, the above example illustrates how quality assessment can lead to deserved rewards for both staff and students. It seems clear that this hitherto relatively unnoticed department had benefited considerably from quality assessment in three of the ways discussed previously in this chapter – in terms of reputation, income and influence.

Conclusion

Westerheijden has suggested that there is an inherent contradiction in quality assessment linked to rewards (Westerheijden, 1990). If there are real rewards and punishments attached to the results of assessment, then a 'game' of compliance may result and the potential benefits of learning, self-criticism and improvement may all be foregone. Trow has made a largely similar point (Trow, 1996). On the other hand, if quality assessment has no consequences – if there are neither rewards nor punishments attendant upon its outcomes – then why should anyone take it seriously?

This chapter has described a more complex situation. Rewards can themselves lead to change and improvement, for example through enhanced morale and motivation, through greater productivity, occasionally through increased funding. The crucial issue must surely lie with what is rewarded by any particular assessment system. The more formalistic accreditation-type assessment systems may achieve less in terms of institutional change than systems which differentiate more subtly and on more process-related criteria and which involve greater critical appraisal by staff within the institution.

Even here, there are contrary examples. The authors of one of the Hungarian case studies writes that

> The accreditation, that is the first overall expert external evaluation, was a milestone in the life of the college. It was in fact a forced SWOT analysis of the quality of staff, courses, teaching, research, management, students and infrastructure.
>
> (Filep, 1998: 11)

Here, it was the nature of the evaluation process leading up to accreditation, rather than the accreditation act itself, which appears to have been valuable. Yet the positive effect on an institution of gaining a desired formal status, even without the benefits of the linked evaluation process, should not be underestimated, particularly if it represents a collective achievement by the members of the institution rather than the result of political diktat.

The conclusion must be that there appears no sound reason for failing to reward the results of quality assessment, although not necessarily with increased funding. Indeed, it seems difficult to avoid at least some modest rewards of reputation and influence – or, indeed, sheer collective relief – arising from a successful assessment outcome. By the same token, it may be impossible to avoid some element of punishment arising from an unsuccessful outcome – demoralization, loss of reputation – even if concrete penalties are not involved.

As the Mexican experiences indicate, rewards do not have to reside in external assessment. They can also be a positive feature of internal assessment arrangements, even though there are also a whole host of political and cultural factors that enter into consideration at the institutional level.

To summarise, we have considered in this chapter how quality assessment can lead to rewards through enhanced reputation, status allocation, increased funding and greater influence. In turn, these rewards can result in increased morale among staff and students and in higher levels of productivity. By the same token, quality assessment can also lead to the obverse of all these benefits when a bad result obtains.

8

Impact of Quality Assessment through Changing Policies and Structures

Introduction

In Chapter 7 we suggested that policy and structural changes within institutions were likely to occur in response both to the recommendations contained in assessment reports and to the overall nature of the external quality assessment methodology. The examples that will be provided in this chapter in part confirm this proposition, but they also serve to remind us of the role which assessment plays in the everyday activities of managing universities. Many of the IMHE case studies described ad hoc assessment activities initiated by an institution in order to deal with internal issues and problems. In such cases, the need for some kind of change had already been agreed (at least by some of the participants) and the purpose of the assessment was to determine the precise nature of the change.

Assessment activities undertaken as part of the requirements of external quality agencies had a more complex relationship to change within institutions. Westerheijden and Maassen (1998) have referred to three types of use of external assessment results by decision-makers in higher education institutions: active use, passive use and no use. Active use refers to cases where decisions are made on the basis of assessment outcomes. Passive use refers to cases where, although decisions are not linked directly to assessment outcomes, they are 'acknowledged in the evaluated organization's decision-making processes, for example by dissemination of the evaluation report, (formal) discussions about it etc.' (Westerheijden and Maassen, 1998: 35). The IMHE case studies suggest that decisions are rarely taken entirely on the basis of assessment outcomes (unless these outcomes are both dramatic and negative), but that such outcomes can play a contributory part in decisions. This is something more than Westerheijden and Maassen's 'passive use' as dissemination and discussion do not of themselves imply that actions are taken, even indirectly, as a result of assessment. In practice, assessment outcomes become factors to be deployed in the decision-making process, arguments to be used in favour of certain kinds of actions, considerations which can strengthen the position of some groups against others. They are more likely to lead to action when such action does not run counter to the interests of powerful groups within the institution. In other words, the impact of quality assessment depends on institutional context. For example, an institution with a long tradition of faculty autonomy is unlikely to respond positively to external assessment recommendations which call for stronger institutional policies at the centre.

Do institutional policies matter?

This brings us to institutional policies and structures, which are the focus of this chapter. Institutional structure refers to ways in which basic units – in Becher and Kogan's terms, departments, research centres, faculties and institutes – are organized and to the kinds of powers which are exercised by such units (Becher and Kogan, 1992). Curriculum structures tend to reflect the organizational structure of units but do not always do so, particularly when significant organizational power rests at the centre of the institution. Policies exist and are determined at both institutional and basic unit levels and cover academic matters (e.g. student assessment, research) and non-academic matters (e.g. finance, personnel).

It might be supposed, therefore, that it is by affecting institutional policies and structures that quality assessment is able to make its greatest impact. This, however, begs the question of the effectiveness of institutional policies and structures in determining the activities of individual staff members. The tradition of autonomy of individual academics remains strong in many higher education institutions. The authority and reputation of key figures in the institution can enable them to subvert formal institutional policies and structures. The power of, and external loyalties towards, subject disciplines can be a more important factor in determining action at the basic unit level than anything handed down from the institutional centre. All of this is well known and extensively documented in analyses of higher education organizations (e.g. Clark, 1983; Becher, 1989; Becher and Kogan, 1992). It is important to bear it in mind in considering the IMHE case studies for two reasons, one of which could serve to limit the impact of quality assessment and one of which could serve to heighten it.

First, there are circumstances in which impact through structures and policies is likely to be limited. We noted in Chapter 1 that most of the IMHE case studies had been written by people connected with the administration of their institutions, so that their perspectives tended to be those of the centre rather than those of basic units. These perspectives accord more importance to institutional policies and structures than would be found among teaching staff in departments and research units.[1] In recognizing this potential bias in our own study, we need to be aware of the danger of according too much weight to policies and structures and of overstating their importance in the organizational life of the institution. Where institutional levels of decision-making are weak and basic units possess considerable autonomy from the centre, one of the principal mechanisms through which quality assessment can make an impact is largely removed. In other words, if institutional policies and structures have only a weak relationship to what goes on in practice in the institution, then the changes they promote will be largely window-dressing, giving rise to compliance without change. The importance of quality assessment through policies and structures could be negligible in such circumstances.

However, there are also circumstances in which the impact of quality assessment through changing policies and structures can be very strong. If an external quality assessment is sufficiently far-reaching, if it is based on managerial values of accountability and is accompanied by some real powers to enforce them, then it can provide a strong impetus towards strengthening the central authority of an institution over that of its basic units, towards emphasizing the importance of institutional-level policies and towards the introduction of effective internal monitoring and accountability procedures to ensure that the policies are actually implemented. In such cases, quality assessment can change the essential character of a higher education institution. It might be hypothesized that external quality assessment and evaluation activities would be more likely to have these kinds of effects than internal assessment activities. The latter would be more likely to perpetuate the status quo of existing structures and authority.

In this chapter we shall try to maintain a distinction between impacts on structures and policies which are *fundamental* to the life and organization of the institution, i.e. those that change the balance of power and organizational values – what Clark has described as 'fundamental change' within a higher education institution (Clark, 1983) – and those which are substantive but more narrowly focused on a particular area of policy or part of the institution. In the next section, we consider the latter case, examples of which can be found in most of the IMHE case studies. The subsequent section looks at some of the less frequent examples of cases where quality assessment appears to be associated with more fundamental shifts in policy-making and the organizational structures which support it. The final section of the chapter considers some related themes of information, institutional quality management and decision-making.

Substantive policy changes in institutions

The two Mexican case studies provide useful instances of the different kinds of impact of quality assessment. Impacts through reward at the Autonomous National University of Mexico were described in Chapter 7. The same university provides two examples of the impact of quality assessment on substantive policies: in the School of Engineering and, university-wide, in its graduate studies. In both cases, assessment activities were undertaken for internal reasons, although external inputs were made to the evaluation processes.

In the case of the School of Engineering, the assessment was the latest in a series of periodic reviews of curricula and organization undertaken within the school. Among the inputs to the assessment were an alumni study, a pan-American study, international accreditation requirements and national evaluation guidelines in engineering (Rojo *et al.*, 1998). We described the methods used in this assessment in Chapter 6.

The assessment appears to have pulled no punches. The engineering programmes were found to be 'outdated, lacking clarity regarding the objectives of the study plan, with content repetition, inadequate use of basic sciences, and an imbalance between core and peripheral topics' (Rojo *et al.*, 1998: 28). Actions taken as a result of the evaluation are discussed in the case study under the headings of changes in academic governance (with an enhanced role for external advisory committees), curricular changes (with 11 new study plans and curricula) and changes in academic culture (a greater voice for academics and students).

Whereas the engineering assessment was part of a regular evaluation cycle, the review of graduate education was a one-off exercise, prompted by a widespread view within the university that individual graduate programmes were too isolated. Reviews of the various graduate programmes were conducted between 1989 and 1995 by collegiate bodies of university members with inputs by Mexican and foreign external groups. Many curricula and organizational changes occurred as a result of these assessments. In addition, in December 1995, the university council approved new general rules for graduate studies at the university, including

- the articulation and integration of various academic university entities (faculties, schools, institutes, centres) and their academic personnel, in joint and shared graduate programmes;
- the creation of new collegiate bodies to design, propose and conduct specific doctoral and masters programmes;
- the strengthening of the tutorial system;
- the introduction of flexibility to shape a graduate programme to each student's needs, while ensuring quality;
- the opening of new graduate study opportunities (both interdisciplinary and multidisciplinary), thus providing for growth in graduate studies according to the institution's potential and national needs.

The pivotal role of assessment in institutional change is emphasized by these two Mexican examples: not assessment required by external bodies but assessment which is an integral part of institutional decision-making and policy formation.

Many other examples of this kind of regular assessment and evaluation linked to institutional change policies can be found in the IMHE case studies. In the case of the Free University of Brussels, the authors provide five examples of evaluation activities within the university under the headings of teaching staff recruitment and tenure; student appraisals of teaching performance; skill development of administrative and technical staff; selection and funding of research projects; and continuing and post-university training. More recently, the university has sought to integrate much of its separate evaluation activity into an overall assessment plan. This will focus on programmes and require skills profiles, content descriptions and syntheses of programme information in an attempt to achieve overall consistency across the institution. As with the Mexican examples, evaluations within Brussels have been self-initiated (Bodson, 1998).

In Finland, at the University of Helsinki, a number of internally initiated evaluations have been carried out. Some of the methods used at faculty level were described in Chapter 6. Their impacts are described by the case-study authors as follows:

> On the basis of the evaluations, many practical measures have been planned and implemented, and these seem to be of great practical significance, at least in terms of improving the framework of university operations. For example, methods of assessing the quality of teaching have been developed and put into use. Wide-ranging personnel development programmes have been planned based on the feedback obtained in these assessments. Assessments of the quality of teaching have also been reflected in the sometimes far-reaching curriculum reforms . . . The benefits of the evaluations can also be seen in many areas of strategic planning, such as in the formation of the University's objectives and general policy aims and in its research policy. Thus, we can conclude that nearly all of the evaluation projects described in this report have been followed by reforms in the corresponding areas.
>
> (Hyvärinen *et al.*, 1998: 25)

The case studies referred to so far in this section have been drawn from countries which at the time did not possess fully operational external quality assessment systems. The case study of Uppsala in Sweden was prepared when a national assessment system was being introduced, although its procedures and methods were not then known. However, the evaluation activities described in the Uppsala case study might be regarded as having been undertaken to some extent in anticipation of the introduction of a national system. What is interesting about this case study is the 'bottom-up' approach to policy-making which it describes. Faculties have traditionally possessed considerable autonomy at Uppsala and this was not contested in the university's approach to evaluation. Different faculties adopted very different approaches to evaluation and quality management but some common problems were nevertheless identified to which collective university solutions might be sought. The problems in question related to seven areas: departmental self-assessment; departmental management; conditions for students; equal opportunities; the potential of information technology; postgraduate research training; and international relations. The university's quality committee commissioned projects in each of these areas. The results of these projects appeared unlikely to shape overall institutional policies but were expected to feed into policy and practice in individual departments, respecting disciplinary conditions and traditions. Collaboration between departments has been an important feature of these quality assessment activities (Engwall, 1997).

France has the longest-established system of external evaluation in Europe through its National Evaluation Committee, but many of the evaluation activities described in the French case studies have been internally initiated, albeit in a context in which external evaluation requirements are an ever-present feature. Internal evaluation activities at the University of the Social Sciences, Toulouse I are described under the headings of admission, guidance and information; education and teaching; relations with the world of work; research; and personnel management. In the latter case, training for administrators in the use of information technology has been introduced and has made it possible to redefine staff members' duties so that they can carry out a more complex set of administrative tasks under their own initiatives (Saint-Girons and Vincens, 1998: 15).

Some of the evaluation activity undertaken internally at Toulouse might accord with Westerheijden and Maassen's concept of 'passive use' in that direct links to institutional change and policy formation are not always clear. Nevertheless, the widespread occurrence of innovation and change in the university is well documented in the case study and it is reasonable to infer that evaluation has played its part in generating it.

The emphasis placed so far in this section on the impact of internally initiated activities should not be taken to imply an absence of impact by external evaluation. Toulouse had experienced a National Evaluation Committee (Comité National d'Évaluation – CNE) evaluation in 1994 which had led, inter alia, to the closing of two departments, to the creation of a Common Documentation Service in line with national library regulations, to the reorganization of continuing training provision, and to a greater focus in research on law. These and other changes introduced as a result of the CNE evaluation reflect both direct and indirect responses to the recommendations made by the CNE.

At the Louis Pasteur University in Strasbourg, a wide range of internal and external evaluations are described and their inputs to university policy-making are outlined in respect of the internal organization of the university (e.g. the creation of the School and Observatory for Earth Sciences and the Faculty of Life Sciences out of the School and Observatory for Geophysics and the Education/Training and Research Unit for Life and Earth Sciences), the development of library policy, and changes in employment and staff policy. Several of these changes could be related back to CNE recommendations made in 1986 (Cheminat and Hoffert, 1998).

The difficulty of distinguishing clearly between the respective impacts of internal and external quality assessment and evaluation activities is drawn out in the final two institutional case studies to be referred to in this section. The issue is set out clearly by the author of the Cardiff University of Wales case study:

> It is difficult *directly* to attribute the impact of external quality requirements on all the recent changes occurring at structural, cultural, curriculum and governance levels within the University, because many would have happened in any event.
>
> (Daniels, 1998: 13)

The author goes on to locate many of the changes taking place within her university as responses to the kinds of contextual factors discussed in Chapters 3 and

4. Within Cardiff, a 35 per cent increase in student numbers over five years, modularization of the curriculum and increased expectations on behalf of students are among the more important recent changes. What the recent changes in Cardiff indicate is the extensive development in internal quality management systems in some institutions. Recent changes in structural, cultural, curriculum and governance levels within the university are described in the case study under six main headings: new committees; new managers; change of role of heads of departments; deployment of resources; staff development practices; and approaches to teaching and learning. Changes in each of the areas relate to many factors but quality issues have evidently been important. New committees include an Academic Quality Assurance Committee and a Teaching and Learning Committee. New managers include a Director of Registry and Academic Secretary who is responsible, inter alia, for Quality Support and Development, a Pro Vice-Chancellor for Teaching and Learning, and a Teaching Quality Assessment Officer. Following an external audit report, formalized written staff development policies are required of all departments. A university-wide teaching and learning policy was approved in 1996.

These changes cannot be related to a single external or internal cause. Nor are their implications for the work of staff and students in the university's academic departments entirely clear. The caveats at the beginning of this chapter about the problems of assessing impact are particularly relevant here. When so much seems to be changing, the role of specific factors and the significance of particular changes may be difficult to discern: their importance is liable to be either exaggerated or underestimated.

The final case study has already been discussed in Chapter 4, and the details will not therefore be repeated here. It concerns the experiences of the University of Amsterdam and, in particular, the impact of external assessment on the Faculty of Psychology and the Faculty of Economic Sciences and Econometrics. The report provides a useful example of the ways in which institutional contextual factors can mediate the impact of external assessment. In the case of the latter faculty,

> Publication of the assessment's outcome did not, however, initiate the pursuit of improvements in the faculty's general functioning. A crisis within the faculty administration caused the negative educational assessment to fade into the background.
>
> (de Klerk *et al.*, 1998: 16)

Institutional factors can place quality assessment outcomes in the foreground or in the background. The Amsterdam case study offers an interesting illustration of how internal assessment activities can be more critical and more effective in directing change than external assessments. Universities are capable of identifying their own problems and doing something about them. In the case of economics, subsequent improvements were 'not dictated by the results of the external assessment' but occurred as part of the general 'internal recovery' of the faculty. The case-study authors make their own interesting conclusions:

(i)   If an institution in crisis, weak management, and a lack of social cohesion within the organization inhibit realizing the ideal process of assessment . . ., a relatively friction-less general situation of an institution, strong departmental management and involvement with the institution as a whole probably stimulate such assessment.

(ii)   Some kind of stimulus is necessary to initiate such a process. In the Faculty of Economic Sciences and Econometrics, the crisis provided a general impulse for change. This factor may be present in trends within higher education in this situation (and for all institutions). In contrast to the situation at the beginning of the decade (characterized by the massive increase in student enrolment), universities and faculties now face a serious decline in the number of students. Combined with the public accessibility of assessment reports, this situation inspires worry about the faculty's external (i.e. market) reputation and thus concern for the outcome of the assessments.

(de Klerk *et al.*, 1998: 19)

The Amsterdam case lends support to one of the main points we have been arguing in this book. The impact of quality assessment – however carried out and whether external or internal – is largely dependent on institutional context, which is in turn heavily dependent on national context. The question is raised, therefore, of whether quality assessment can itself help to produce fundamental changes in institutional structures and policies which may in turn provide a more receptive context for the outcomes of future assessment activities.

Fundamental changes in policy-making and organizational structure

If we consider some of the changes which were taking place in Cardiff, we can identify some of the characteristics of the more fundamental changes in policy and structure occurring in higher education institutions. Thus, department boards 'equivalent to senior management teams' *advise* the head of department on 'policy issues, strategic development and resourcing'. Head of department roles and responsibilities are 'more clearly defined' and mark a 'move away from collegiate to managerial role'. These familiar moves to more explicit management responsibilities in higher education institutions appear to enhance the likelihood that quality assessment reports will be acted upon. Thus, at Cardiff, one of the outcomes of the university's internal quality review procedures is *a management report*

which contains an evaluation of the Department's strengths and weaknesses, an assessment of its objectives and the extent to which they are being met . . .

Implementation of any recommendations approved by appropriate Committees of the University is monitored by the Academic Quality Assurance Committee . . . The Department comments on the Report and can be asked to provide progress reports on implementation of improvements.

After the (internal) review one of the members of the Review Panel is designated to maintain contact with the Department in respect of quality-related matters. A year after, the same individual meets formally with the Head of Department and senior colleagues to advise the relevant committees on the progress made in the Department since the Internal Quality Review took place. Thus the quality loop is completed.

(Daniels, 1998: 11)

In this way, heads are held accountable to the rest of the university for the activities of their departments. In theory at least, the committees and policies of the university ensure that quality assessment outcomes are acted upon. The implication is that the autonomy of the basic departmental unit is weakened. University-level policies exist on matters which were previously left to departmental discretion and internal accountability structures ensure that these policies are implemented.

The Australian cases in the IMHE study provide the most developed examples of organizational structures designed to introduce greater managerialism and formalism.

The author of the Monash case study sets the scene:

It should be pointed out that the 'quality' movement is only one of a number of developments affecting management and decision-making processes in Australian universities. There has been much talk in recent years of the 'corporatization' of these institutions, seen by critics as an attack on traditional collegiate values and by proponents as a necessary injection of hard-headed business thinking into organizations which have been hamstrung in their response to change by cumbersome and reactionary procedures. A major review of the management of universities has just been announced by the Commonwealth government and placed firmly in its broader agenda of a national strategy for enhancing competitiveness and efficiency.

(Baldwin, 1997: 11)

In such an organizational context, quality assessment becomes more closely allied to, and is frequently seen as the first stage of, planning processes. It is a short step from evaluation and planning – and the performance data they generate – to the introduction of incentive schemes. The latter have existed at Monash for some time in relation to research. At the time the case study was written, an incentive scheme with regard to teaching was also about to be introduced.

It is worth remembering (see Chapter 3) that Australia's various experiments in national quality assessment have been funding-related. This approach also appears to have been adopted within some of its higher education institutions as part of a movement to create a more market-oriented higher education system.

Changes in the external environment can provide opportunities for managers of institutions to introduce far-reaching internal changes. Thus, at the University of Newcastle in Australia,

From the point of view of the Vice-Chancellor of the time, the (external) quality rounds represented an invaluable opportunity to attempt to change both culture and practice in an institution which had not previously set great value on the formal processes of quality assurance. The national quality assurance process, therefore, was 'harnessed and ridden' for all it was worth to assist the process of change management. It is likely that the then Vice-Chancellor would have been interested in the identification of cost savings as well as the winning of reward funds from the quality assurance process.

(Lester, 1998: 19)

Similar examples of management uses of quality assessment have been reported elsewhere (e.g. Brennan, Frederiks and Shah, 1997) and, indeed, a substantial literature on total quality management has emphasized the central role of quality assessment in institutional management and change in organizations of all kinds (Dill, 1995; Kells, 1995).

Do the far-reaching, institutionally managed quality systems being developed by Australian universities represent a triumph of business approaches to the running of universities and do they provide lessons for universities elsewhere? Elaborate institutional quality systems, while strengthening institutional management, need a reasonably strong central management in the first place if they are to be introduced successfully. This appears to have been present in the Australian universities in question and, to a large extent, in those British universities which provided case studies. External factors – particularly connected with funding – have encouraged greater institutional control in several other countries (Finland and Mexico are examples from the IMHE study) and this has facilitated the promotion of institution-wide quality systems and their integration into management and decision-making.

This relationship between quality assessment and central institutional management is discussed in the case study of the University of Jyväskylä in Finland. The university had undertaken a 'total evaluation' as a national pilot project prior to the introduction of a national quality system. Its links to new style management thinking within the university are revealed in this extract from the case-study report.

After the total evaluation, the restructuring of TTS-plans (university planning system) in different hierarchical levels of the university had had important consequences. All planning documents are now written in an evaluative and even in an innovative style. New plans contain very detailed descriptions of development activities, statistics on various academic outputs and information on research priority areas. The old laconic statistical and formal administrative style of the documents has changed into innovative and reflexive style signifying some kind of cultural change in the university administration from old style bureaucracy to modern style reflexive and responsive planning and coordination of various activities.

Total evaluation has supported the understanding of Jyväskylä University as a local production unit of academic degrees, whereas the scholarly dimension that combines academic communities into global academic communities of scholars is weakening.

(Välimaa *et al.*, 1998: 23)

Are such changes about institutional style or substance? A questionnaire survey of departmental heads at Jyväskylä suggests the former:

> impacts caused by the total evaluation are not seen clearly at the departmental level. General picture is that total evaluation has not changed departmental decision-making or academic activities. This supports the notions gained in interviews of academics: total evaluation was a single episode that did not change the activities of academics or basic units.

(Välimaa *et al.*, 1998: 25)

The relative invisibility of impacts of quality assessment at the level of basic units can be related to the contrasts between direct and indirect impact reviewed in Chapter 7. In the Jyväskylä case study, direct impacts are seen to take place at the institutional level (reorganization of some departments; introduction of a new planning and evaluation cycle connected to 'management by results') and indirect changes at the level of the academic basic units (curricular changes and new research priorities).

The authors of the Jyväskylä evaluation are in no doubt that the changes amount to a significant shift in the location of power within the university.

> In summary the university centre is the greatest benefitor of total evaluation . . . Central administration has become more powerful for two reasons: first, rhetorically, central administration has defined what is the mission of the university. Self-evaluation and peer review have served as a useful document that has been used in the argumentation. Referring to the peer report, the university central administration has been able to define the 'real problems' thus defining what is the functional nature of the university. Second, quality assessment has become an instrument for institutional administration, and it has been made part of the annual planning cycle of the university. It produces information and ideas that are developed in faculties and central administration into development projects. This way, total evaluation has strengthened the role of the central administration: it has more power.

(Välimaa *et al.*, 1998: 29)

In some universities at least, the introduction of institutional quality management systems appears to be part of major organizational changes which entail a fundamental shift in authority from basic academic units to the administrative centre of the institution. The purpose of such shifts is well summed up in the case study of the University of Western Sydney, Nepean where the author states: 'Hopefully this restructuring will result in greater accountability at lower levels of the organization and an appropriate monitoring of quality control issues' (Mikol, 1998: 36).

Accountability within higher education institutions is closely linked to the accountability required from institutions by the state. These are considered further in the final section of this chapter.

Accountability, information and quality assurance

One of the most visible impacts of external quality management systems on higher education institutions is the generation of internal quality management systems. In part, these are necessary in order to ensure institutional success in the external systems, and in part to enable the institution to succeed in an external environment marked by funding cuts and greater competition. Institutions need to know what they are good at, need to be able to demonstrate this knowledge convincingly to others, and need to improve efficiency without sacrifice of quality. In these circumstances, quality management becomes firmly integrated into general management processes; the outcomes of quality assessment become important parts of management information; and quality management and assessment is 'owned' by the administration, which accordingly devises quality systems for implementation across the whole institution.

Some national systems encourage these sorts of developments more than others. In France, the necessity for each institution to prepare a four-year development plan as the basis for its contract with government (on which future funding is dependent) has given a major impetus to the collection of information about all aspects of the work of the institution, and to evaluation based on this information, all in relation to the negotiating process with the ministry. Other external requirements come from the National Evaluation Committee and the national Costs Observatory for Higher Education.

What does this mean in practice for an institution? At the University of Lille III – Charles de Gaulle,

> the President's office expanded and, in addition to the inevitable secretariat, largely turned itself into an evaluation and perspectives unit with:
> - a statistician;
> - project officers who either took responsibility for strategic tasks assisting in decision-making or carried out 'field studies' into the circulation of information, the management of future staffing needs and other equally important matters;
> - a co-ordinator for appeals for tenders and other national and international programmes.
>
> (Losfeld and Verin, 1998: 18)

The centrality of information to all aspects of institutional management is emphasized in the following extract of a memorandum from the president of the University of Lille III, dated April 1996, as quoted in the case-study report.

> Perfect circulation of information is a corollary of the management of complexity, which insists that no decision shall be taken, at whatever level,

without thought being given to what interactions there are, or may be, with other component units or with the entire University.

(Losfeld and Verin, 1998: 18)

Other management actions taken at Lille III have included the development of indicators of the match between teaching resources and pedagogical objectives, an inventory of competences aimed at achieving quality, a budget designed to achieve objectives and to devolve greater responsibility to the basic units of the university, the creation of a Resource Centre for Pedagogical Research and Innovation, and an examination of the implications for the university of the greater administrative use of information technology and of planning and the use of space. All of these actions have as their driving force the objective of marrying quality, management and decision-making, the achievement of which has redefined relationships between the 'academic complex' of the university and its central administration and services.

Evaluation thus plays an increasing part in the management of higher education institutions. In so doing, it helps secure greater legitimacy with outside audiences and contributes towards the achievement of accountability to funders and other stakeholders. Both functions are described in the case study of Ca' Foscari University of Venice.

. . . evaluation plays a role that goes well beyond its practical success in affecting research, teaching or administrative activities in the university. It reassures the broader social and institutional audience that the university is undertaking an effort of being more rational, of making its output more transparent and of managing more efficiently its resources.

(Warglien and Savoia, 1998: 18)

Conclusion

It is not easy to separate cause from effect. In some higher education institutions, the creation of a comprehensive internal system of quality management is part of more fundamental changes in institutional management and decision-making. Central to these is the systematic collection of greater amounts of information about all aspects of the institution and the use of such information to ascertain whether performance objectives have been met. Such developments can generally be related to changing relationships between higher education and the state which call for explicit accountability based upon transparency of decision-making and evidence. In some countries, they also represent responses to increasing market competition between institutions. External quality assessment systems feed into the creation of these internal structures and policies but they do not generally seem to be fundamental to them. They affect the content and methods of internal systems which would need to exist for other reasons.

The requirements of external accountability do not seem to be met by responses of compliance in the majority of institutions. They are more likely to generate major internal managerial and structural change: internal account-ability systems to mirror external systems. These are part of the necessary strat-egies and mechanisms by which institutions negotiate their relationship with an ever more complex external environment. It is the general complexity of the environment, rather than the specific impact of external quality assessment sys-tems, which seems to be the prime generator of fundamental structural and policy changes within institutions. Assessment activities – internal or external – may lead to substantive policy changes in particular parts of an institution, but the extent of their impact is heavily dependent upon the contextual features of the institution.

Note

1. Compare, for example, a recent study which is more strongly based on basic unit per-spectives (Bauer and Henkel, 1998).

9

Impact of Quality Assessment through Changing Cultures

Introduction

Culture both facilitates and blocks change. The traditional features of higher education institutions – loosely coupled basic units, a high degree of professional autonomy for the people who work in them, highly specialized work roles – ensure an important role for cultural factors in determining the inner workings of these organizations. Culture encompasses how people feel about themselves, their work, their institutions. It embraces both values, attitudes and behaviour. And, above all, it is shared. Clark describes the role of culture as follows:

> All major social entities have a symbolic side, a culture as well as a social structure, some shared accounts and common beliefs that help define for participants who they are, what they are doing, why they are doing it, and whether they have been blessed or cursed.
>
> (Clark, 1983: 72)

This chapter will look at the impact of quality management and assessment on the cultures of higher education institutions. In attempting to do so, we shall again draw on the IMHE study although, as we have previously noted, the methodology of the study contains some weaknesses which limit the reliance we can place on it in the cultural domain. In Chapter 1, we remarked that a majority of the case studies had been written by people located in central administrative units of their institutions and who, in writing about those institutions as a whole, would almost inevitably adopt a management perspective. This was not a serious drawback in looking at methods of quality management or at institutional structures and rewards. The establishment of a new committee, a major change in curriculum, a change in the ways in which salaries are determined, are reasonably incontrovertible facts. The meanings which they have for the people who are affected by them are not so clear.

Yet cultural factors are intimately bound up with the matters we have been discussing in the two preceding chapters. The notion of a reward entails an assumption about values. The once ambitious staff member who receives a certificate or medal as a reward for 25 years of long service may be thrown into depression by this reminder of age and failure to achieve youthful aspirations. And the value placed on a financial reward will also vary, according to life-style, personal priorities and the existing financial circumstances of the individual concerned. Some changes in policy and structure brook no resistance from culture – if your department is closed down, culture provides no defence. But curriculum changes to support new institutional missions and objectives can be subverted for a long time by staff who prefer to cling to established habits and to recycle their old lectures.

The anthropologist Mary Douglas has written aptly for our purposes, that 'an institution cannot have purposes . . . Only individuals can intend, plan consciously, and contrive oblique strategies' (Douglas, 1986: 92, quoted in Maassen, 1996).

This is a useful reminder, in these times of corporatism in the management of university affairs, of the importance of the distribution of power within higher education institutions. As an individual lecturer might remark: 'the university president can decide on the mission; I'll decide on what I teach my students'. It is people, not organizations who have purposes and these are frequently in conflict with each other.

It is the potential of quality management to break this 'happy anarchy' of university life that makes it so significant to the development of universities. In some forms of quality management at least, our lecturer will no longer have such freedom to decide what to teach, nor how to teach, nor how to assess the students. The relationship between these activities and wider institutional, and perhaps national, notions of mission and objectives will be subject to regular scrutiny and accountability. As we noted in Chapter 1, it is the linkage of the macro policies of governments and institutions to the micro practices of staff and students that makes quality management and assessment so interesting (and so worrying, depending on one's point of view).

In the rest of this chapter, we shall consider some of the problems entailed in the analysis of culture before going on to discuss its role in the processes of quality management and institutional change which have been the subject of the rest of this book. We will then select a number of examples from the IMHE case studies which illustrate the effects of culture in mediating the impact of quality management and assessment in higher education institutions.

Perspectives on culture

Culture has a content and a membership. Within higher education, both features have tended to be defined in terms of subject communities, and the values and social organization of the subject or disciplinary group have been related to the epistemological properties of the subject/discipline (Biglan, 1973; Collins, 1975; Becher, 1989). Overlapping this has been a notion of institutional culture (Clark, 1970 and 1972; Becher and Kogan, 1992) and a general attention to organizational levels such as we discussed in Chapter 7.

A useful and more formal way of considering the analysis of culture is provided by Mary Douglas. Douglas uses two dimensions to distinguish different aspects of an individual's involvement in social life, namely 'group' and 'grid'. Group refers to the strength of group boundaries while grid refers to the intensity of the external rules and regulations imposed upon an individual (Douglas, 1982: 190–2). The point to note here is that from this perspective culture is intimately bound up with structure. Changes in group boundaries and in the strength of the external 'rules' to which the group is subject will constitute changes to culture.

Combining the two dimensions of group and grid in various ways, Douglas suggests four types of social culture: hierarchy, fatalism, egalitarianism and individualism. In a recent work, Maassen has described these four types as follows:

> Hierarchy refers to a situation in which an individual's social life is characterized by strong group boundaries and intense rules and regulations. Individuals who are not a member of a group while at the same time being subject to intense, binding prescriptions produce fatalistic social relations. Strong group boundaries and weak external prescriptions refer to an egalitarian social context. Finally, individuals who are neither bound by intense external rules and regulations exemplify individualistic social relations.
>
> (Maassen, 1996: 29–30)

In higher education institutions, a weakening of boundaries between basic units such as we see with the growth of multidisciplinarity and the centralization of decision-making would tend to produce cultures of fatalism or individualism among staff: fatalism in cases where rules and regulations are strong and individualism where rules and regulations are weak.

Maassen suggests that these cultural types can be regarded as distinctive 'ways of life': 'A way of life is interpreted as a viable combination of social relations on the one hand and cultural bias, i.e. shared values and beliefs, on the other' (Maassen, 1996: 30). Maassen and others have suggested that a fifth type should be added to the four proposed by Douglas. This is 'autonomy' which refers to the case of individuals who withdraw from social involvement altogether (p. 77).

The question which this analytic approach poses for the kinds of changes which are taking place in higher education institutions is whether or not they constitute a transition for their members from one way of life to another. The answer to this question, for Maassen, is to be found in two indicators: the amount of freedom a person has to operate individually, and the amount of control a person has over his or her own social context. He goes on to elaborate these indicators in terms of the level of competition, the intensity of evaluation and the extent of decentralization that is taking place in higher education institutions (Maassen, 1996: 97–8).

On the basis of this model, it might seem that quality management and assessment are associated with some fairly fundamental cultural changes in many of the IMHE case-study institutions. Both the changing contexts – growth, diversity, funding cuts, organizational restructuring – and the methods of quality assessment themselves are reducing the freedoms of individual academics.

However, this conclusion would, we contend, be premature. It neglects two things. The first is the content of culture: the values and beliefs which comprise it. The second is the representation of higher education cultures as primarily the property of the staff of institutions, to the neglect of student culture.

At this point, we need to return to the typology of values of quality assessment described in Chapter 2. The four types were the academic (subject focus – knowledge and curricula), the managerial (institutional focus – policies and procedures), the pedagogic (people focus – skills and competences) and the employment related (output focus – graduate standards/learning outcomes). As we saw in Chapter 5, different national systems of quality assessment emphasize different types. Where there is compatibility between the values of quality assessment and the values of the academic culture, there is no reason to believe that the kinds of structural changes discussed in Chapter 8 and in the Douglas/Maassen analysis above will necessarily be associated with changes in culture. Indeed, the values and behaviours associated with the culture might be strengthened.

To take a concrete example, which is illustrated in the IMHE case studies and more widely, external quality assessment at the subject level within institutions which uses academic peers from the subject group may serve to strengthen the subject culture within the individual institution and act as a defence against, for example, managerial and labour market pressures to change. Similarly, institutions or subject groups with strong linkages to the labour market and a focus on employability will find little difficulty with quality management and assessment approaches which stress these same values.

A crucial question, therefore, is whether quality assessment – whether at national or institutional levels – is uniform in approach and homogeneous in the values it represents or diverse in respecting alternative values across the system or institution. This is partly the 'fitness of' as against the 'fitness for' purpose argument (e.g. Watson, 1997). Even when intentions are benign, there are considerable difficulties in achieving the latter and avoiding the former (deVries, 1996).

Behaviour is, of course, analytically distinct from values. This can be illustrated with respect to subject differences. A study of the impact of quality assessment upon English universities carried out by the authors reported major differences between subjects in the willingness of departments to respond positively to the recommendations made by external peer assessment groups (Brennan, Frederiks, Shah, 1997). In all cases there was a compatibility of values between external and internal subject peers and the assessment process was carried out within the same formal structure of rules and regulations. Where subject cultures appeared to differ were (a) in the homogeneity of the values possessed by the members, and (b) in willingness to obey the external rules and regulations.

The second way in which we want to enter some caveats about the applicability of the Douglas/Maassen model is in relation to the problematic link between the culture of academic life and student culture. The IMHE study has not been concerned with the latter, but its existence, its distinctiveness and its power must at least be acknowledged. It determines quite as much as anything else what is learned in college (see, for example, the extensive literature review undertaken by Pascarella and Terenzini, 1991). To a significant extent, the skills and competencies of graduates are the skills and competencies which students have chosen to acquire while in higher education. To put it another way, the creation of a learning opportunity does not mean that it will be grasped; the setting of course objectives does not mean that they will be achieved.

The capacity of students collectively to undermine the best intentions of national and institutional policies is insufficiently recognized. Governments may want more engineers, and accordingly create more student places, but students may nonetheless fail to enrol. Institutions and employers may collaborate to produce courses geared to labour market needs, but students may confound the intentions of such courses by seeking jobs with different employers and in different labour market sectors.[1] The linkage between macro policies and micro practices breaks down with the autonomy and unpredictability of student behaviour.

Quality assessment and cultural change

Quality assessment can undermine existing academic cultures by weakening the group boundaries within higher education institutions (the 'group' dimension) and by imposing changed rules and regulations over academic work (the 'grid' dimension). What evidence do we have that this is actually happening? It seems fairly incontrovertible that group boundaries are being weakened in some countries and institutions. As decision-making shifts between levels within institutions so too does the capacity of groups to enforce their own norms and values. In Clark's terms, discipline-rooted authority may be replaced by enterprise-based authority or even by system-based authority (Clark, 1983: 110–23).

Such changes may not necessarily be caused by quality management and assessment systems, but such systems can lend force to them. External quality assessment can strengthen authority at the institutional level by placing emphasis on the exercise of responsibility at that level, by scrutinizing internal mechanisms of accountability, and by requiring institution-wide policies and effective strategies for their implementation. This tends to be the Anglo-Saxon approach to quality management and assessment. It is a challenge to the strength of unique disciplinary cultures within institutions. Conversely, external quality assessment systems which operate at the subject level generally embrace and reinforce disciplinary cultures. This is more common in continental European countries.

As we have seen, however, much quality management and assessment activity is undertaken within institutions at the behest of internal institutional authorities. On the whole, these are less likely to challenge the basic cultural values of the institution, although they can be a mechanism for achieving a shift in values from discipline to enterprise level. But, in the latter case, as with external quality assessment, a clash of values and a potential to change or transform cannot be assumed. It depends on local circumstances, contexts and methods.

A weakening of the 'group' dimension renders the institution and its units more open to changes in external rules and regulations, to the imposition of new values (the 'grid' dimension) culminating in a new 'way of life' for the members of the group. There have been several examples of these kind of changes within the IMHE case studies. In many ways the most remarkable was the 'culture of productivity' in the two Mexican universities created by the comprehensive internal systems of individual assessment and reward which had been introduced. In some ways these did not undermine the existing values of academic work: they did not so much influence what was done as how much was done.

Many of the case-study authors reported that the introduction of teaching quality assessment had caused considerably more attention to be given to the teaching function within the institution – to talking about teaching, to monitoring teaching and, by implication, to the teaching act itself. However, some sceptics would argue that time devoted to quality assessment of teaching is at the expense of time devoted to the actual teaching process. And in some countries, such as the United Kingdom, there may be countervailing pressures on staff from research assessment which actually weaken the importance attached to teaching within the culture of the institution.

Quite apart from the valuation that is given to teaching within different academic cultures is the definition of what constitutes 'good' teaching. There were several examples of trends which appeared to weaken disciplinary cultures in this respect. The inclusion, as in the case of the VSNU in the Netherlands, of pedagogic experts and students on visiting committees would seem to dilute the possibility of basic units defining good teaching exclusively in the terms of their own discipline. The widespread introduction of student feedback questionnaires and of internal institution-wide quality management arrangements are also likely to weaken specialist disciplinary definitions of good teaching. Inevitably, perhaps, these developments lead to greater emphasis on matters of technique than on matters of content selection and organization.

The introduction of more explicit rules and regulations governing the teaching process also threatens the individualistic and autonomous options in the Douglas/Maassen cultural types. The recognition that providing education to students is a collective act and responsibility is a consequence of almost any form of quality management. The time spent in writing documents and sitting in committees at least enables people to become much more aware of the content and objectives of each other's courses. The time spent by increasing numbers of academic staff in peer review activities within and outside institutions further diminishes the individualistic and private nature of the teaching process, since experiences are increasingly shared. It is not unreasonable to expect that some improvements in practice will arise from this sharing.

Some of the case-study authors and other writers have referred to the emergence of evaluation cultures in institutions. Certainly, a much greater amount of time is being devoted to evaluation activity than hitherto. Whether this can give rise to a distinctive evaluation culture is another matter. As we have noted, a significant number of the evaluation and quality assessment activities initiated within institutions relate to institutional problems and pressures for change which have their origins outside of quality management processes. Evaluation activity in response to external quality assessment requirements is usually in part a matter of compliance, even if there are other consequences which prove to be of direct benefit. As we remarked in Chapter 4, higher education institutions face two sorts of needs – a need to change and a need to comply. Both types of need generate an increase in quality assessment activity, but as means to ends.

One may question whether this increase in assessment activity in itself implies a significant change in culture? It probably does so when tied into modes of decision-making. An adoption of 'rational' decision-making based on a combination of objectives and evidence gives a central place to evaluation and quality assessment. New forms of relationship between higher education and the state, as in France, are placing greater emphasis on rational decision-making and this feeds down into internal institutional decision-making processes. It can be regarded as part of the culture of managerialism with greater importance attached to values of rationality than – as in more collegial models of decision-making – to consensus and conflict-resolution.

The above discussion has identified increased productivity, greater emphasis on teaching, new definitions of and a more collective approach to teaching, and a more rational and evidence-based approach to decision-making as among the cultural changes taking place in higher education institutions as a result of the introduction of quality management and assessment. The final section of the chapter looks at some concrete examples from the IMHE case studies.

Impact upon institutional cultures in the IMHE case studies

Examples of cultural impact in the case studies centre on two interrelated themes: attitudes to teaching and approaches to decision-making. Both tend to be discussed in an institution-wide context and so to underplay the impact of specific assessments on individual basic units (although the Sheffield Hallam case study reports on the positive and negative effects upon staff morale in different departments). The case studies are concerned more with the impact of quality management systems as a whole rather than with the consequences of individual assessments. Although this emphasis is partly a function of the methodology adopted for the case studies, the gradual and multifaceted nature of cultural change would suggest that culture would be impervious to all but the most dramatic individual quality assessments.

The University of Leuven provides a good example of changing attitudes to teaching which have been promoted by the introduction of assessment systems within the university. These were largely internal systems established in anticipation of the introduction of external requirements. The authors describe the attitude towards teaching within the university prior to the establishment of systematic quality assessment:

the overall impression is that education is regarded as a job to be done and not as a challenge that requires continuous reflection, time and sufficient resources by a large portion of staff members. This may be partly explained by the repetitive nature of aspects of the teaching task, but also by perceptions about the more challenging nature of research and high pressure in this respect.

> (Bellefroid and Elen, 1998: 29–30)

However, the establishment of various internal commissions and initiatives both to review and to improve quality of teaching appeared to have had some impact upon teaching and learning methods:

> Conceptions about learning and instruction at the university level are gradually changing . . . Acknowledgement is growing that learning is the result of activities engaged in by the learner rather than the outcome of instruction. Lecturing while beneficial to some students for a limited set of goals is not generally approved anymore . . . Therefore, the Educational Council supported a number of projects that aim at fostering deep level learning of students through a variety of means.
>
> (Bellefroid and Elen, 1998: 31)

Innovations in the use of technology – notably through developments in computer-assisted instruction – have represented another strand in the university's approach to improving the quality of teaching and learning.

A further example of developments at Leuven can be found in a growing emphasis upon knowledge application. In this case, problems identified during assessments had given rise to a number of development projects in the university.

> Regularly, external and internal quality assessments have pointed to the poor quality of skill-related components of curricula. Summarized, the complaint is that students at the university know a lot but cannot transfer their knowledge to practice and real problems. They do not know how to apply what they have learned.
>
> (Bellefroid and Elen, 1998: 32)

Development work to clarify the functions of various practice-oriented curriculum components was initiated in response to this criticism.

Another event which has occurred at Leuven is the introduction of (optional) training programmes for new professors and assistants.

Taken together, these various initiatives represent an attempt to change the institution's educational philosophy and to make it more visible and explicit: in effect, to change the institutional culture. The authors of the case study express some reservations about its degree of success.

> Mainly unacceptable problems have been made visible and have been addressed. However, the question remains whether in addition to the identification and abolishment of intolerable teaching situations and of the production of nice looking and interesting reports, educational quality has been improved as well.
>
> (Bellefroid and Elen, 1998: 75)

Leuven has an improvement-oriented quality management and assessment system. The authors of the case study review the responses to the experiences of assessment at the different levels within the university. At the level of individual behaviour, a majority of professors have responded positively:

In most cases, individuals have accepted the results and have tried to change their teaching behaviour, improve exercises, produce or select a better course text, make more deliberate decisions about exam questions and exam format. Sometimes the result has been more co-operation between colleagues and better agreement on the subject matter to be covered. In a limited number of cases, evaluation outcomes have induced curricular changes.

(Bellefroid and Elen, 1998: 40)

A more negative account is presented at the department and faculty levels. Here, effects appear to have been minimal and rare. The authors note that the openness to discuss educational experiences between academic staff and between staff and students that occurred during the assessment process was a completely new experience (p. 42). But it was not an experience that seems to be leading to change. A key reason appears to have been the lack of support from deans:

Some of them do not back up the evaluation commissions and seem to fear interviews with faculty members. They do not install systems as to foster and consolidate the initiatives taken by the evaluation commissions. In some cases, deans themselves have been found to be critical about the quality management system.

(Bellefroid and Elen, 1998: 42)

At the institutional level, however, a generally positive picture emerges. Educational matters have become much more visible and are now frequently discussed at university committees and councils. A new post of vice-president for educational matters has been created. Education-related criteria enter into promotion considerations. Deans are now required to submit follow-up reports to the academic council one year after an assessment. The authors of the case study conclude:

This review of effects may be summarized by putting forward that the quality management system resulted in some changes at the micro-level and an increased visibility of education at the macro level. These changes as well as a greater visibility can be considered to be indicators of a new organizational culture that more strongly values education. However, greater visibility has not yet resulted in major policy changes and certainly at the meso-level a lot remains to be done.

(Bellefroid and Elen, 1998: 43)

We have recorded the Leuven experience in some detail because it provides a full account of issues which are also raised elsewhere. Thus, the Cardiff University of Wales case study notes awareness raising across the university in terms of such matters as resources for teaching and for staff development. The Torino Polytechnic case study describes the creation of an extensive institution-wide pedagogic strategy. The Jyväskylä University case-study report notes that 'Thereafter the different efforts to improve one's teaching have become a well-accepted target of academic work' (Välimaa *et al.*, 1998: 24).

One significant effect on teaching of quality assessment at the University of Leuven appears to have been the promotion of an innovative educational philosophy across the university, irrespective of disciplinary cultures. There are also examples, however, where quality assessment appears to strengthen disciplinary cultures. The difference in outcome is a function of assessment methodology and institutional context. An illustration is provided by Sheffield Hallam University in the United Kingdom.

Sheffield Hallam is a new university which has emphasized multidisciplinarity and close links with employment. The impact of external subject-level assessment by subject peers seems to have been to modify the 'service culture' of the university towards more collegiate subject values and norms. Thus,

> One of the most notable features of the impact of quality assessment has been within subject groups. In an institution where recent trends have been towards large programmes, modularity and a flexible approach to student choice, several participants have found that working together within the subject group on quality assessment has emphasized the value of the 'course team' and of a collegiate culture, and that significantly quality enhancement has resulted from concerted efforts towards a common purpose.
>
> (Arnold, 1998: 11)

This strengthening of the subject group through quality assessment can be assisted by the involvement of subject staff in external assessment visits. In some institutions, appointment as an external assessor can be a status indicator in the educational sphere (comparable in importance as a research indicator to presenting a conference paper). The crucial point is whether the framework used in the external assessment process maps onto the basic unit structure of the home institution. Where it does so, external assessment experience is likely to strengthen the subject group and reflect its values. Where it does not, the reverse may be true.

The general picture, however, seems to be that quality assessment supports notions of good teaching which claim either to be universalistic or to be invariant across an institution. Thus, generic criteria are more likely than subject-specific ones to weaken – or at least to be in conflict with – disciplinary cultures. They are also likely to give weight to consumer views of quality and a conception of the university which emphasizes the employment of its graduates and a role of service to society. There is, for example, a very strong employer voice in the external quality system operated by the Danish Evaluation Centre. However, internal institutional evaluation can also be designed to bring external values into the institution. A good example is the University of Lille III – Charles de Gaulle, in France.

The Lille case reveals how notions of accountability, management, curriculum, teaching and quality assessment all come together:

> on the one hand, the university can no longer simply be a place where knowledge is produced for the sake of it, but rather a place where this knowledge is socialized in such a way as to enable various sections of the population to establish themselves in present-day life as well as they can and at whatever level. On the other hand, our management methods must respond to a powerful logic of service and, what is more, one of public service in which we must be simultaneously actors, promoters and guarantors.
>
> (Losfeld and Verin, 1998: 17)

Within Lille (and elsewhere) quality assessment is seen as a tool with which to alter the balance between the intrinsic and the extrinsic functions (van Vught, 1995) of universities, both in teaching and in research. This, for the authors of the Lille III case study, implies

- there is a need for an evaluation of teaching that focuses perhaps on what is taught, but mainly on the sought-for match between a concern for rigorous education (in the subject-based senses) and implied promises of finding employment;
- a powerful linkage between this dual requirement and research work which can only support this requirement if it simultaneously reconciles the same concern for subject rigour and the need to meet major social demands;
- medium-term forward planning of teaching work, which takes account both of developments in the present-day and a wish to break the University's strong identities.

(Losfeld and Verin, 1998: 21)

Such expressions of institutional values may or may not find accord with the values attached to a particular form of external quality assessment. They also may or may not be fully shared by the academic staff of the institution which propounds them. But quality assessment is frequently a way for external values and interests to be brought into the culture of the institution, whether at the behest of institutional management or by an external quality agency acting on the wishes expressed by national governments. Both can provide a challenge to disciplinary cultures and the autonomy of basic units.

Chapter 8 considered aspects of the relationship between quality assessment and the growth of so-called managerialist approaches to decision-making in higher education. At a cultural level as well, several case-study authors have noted a movement away from collegial to managerial roles for positions such as departmental head and dean. Cardiff provides one such case. The imposition of external quality systems, reflecting in the words of the Cardiff case-study author 'a strong mistrust at Government level of an institution's capability to run and manage its own affairs' (Daniels, 1998: 26) can lead to a managerially imposed internal quality system which represents values derived from outside rather than internal values of the institution. The danger here is the generation of what has been described as a 'compliance culture'.

> There is tension too between what the institution views as important in terms of quality assurance and what may be imposed from outside. A somewhat cynical view is that TQA (the external quality system) shames departments into putting systems, processes and structures into place: pressure is being placed on the recalcitrant. The perceived danger is that a compliance culture develops, with the institution and its departments pursuing pathways determined or suggested by external assessors and where compliance with the assessment becomes the objective.
>
> (Daniels, 1998: 26)

A compliance culture can be a response to managerial processes of decision-making in other spheres of university life. It is a variant of the 'fatalism' of the Douglas typology which is claimed to occur when group boundaries are weakened and the intensity of externally imposed rules and regulations increases.

We should emphasize, however, that we do not detect any necessary relationship between quality assessment, managerial decision-making and responses of compliance and fatalism. In some circumstances, the openness of discussion and the accessibility of information which are normal parts of a self-evaluation process can support 'open' collegial decision-making rather than 'closed' managerial decision-making. This appears to have been the case at the faculty level within the Finnish University of Jyväskylä.

> According to the interviews of the faculty personnel total evaluation helped to discuss and define functional problems in an open situation that promoted development-orientation in the faculties. Therefore, the emergence of focused discussion on functional problems is in itself a positive impact of the total evaluation. Furthermore, the seeing of problems also has promoted improvement activities at the faculty level.
>
> (Välimaa *et al.*, 1998: 23)

However, at departmental level a different picture emerged. A survey of staff indicated that the impact of assessment on the departments was slight, with 78 per cent seeing the impact of assessment as either negative or neutral.

> In short, according to the responses of the departmental heads it seems that the evaluation was just one episode in the past, which has not many long-term impacts to their every-day work within their departments.
>
> (Välimaa *et al.*, 1998: 26)

The authors suggest that the discrepancy between the perceptions at the two levels in the university reflected a distinction both between direct and indirect impacts and between measures taken at faculty or university level and changes resulting from these measures at departmental level. This would appear to be a function of the assessment methodology (total evaluation) at Jyväskylä, which was managed centrally in the university. The true impact of the assessment may have been hidden or routinized at the level of the departmental basic unit.

The authors of the Jyväskylä case study detect the emergence of a form of 'evaluation culture' within the university.

> The impact of total evaluation to the development of different curriculum structures has been significant, even though the individual departments have sometimes denied it. Furthermore, total evaluation has made university staff informed of these problems and pushed ahead these development activities . . .
>
> In cultural terms, we see the nature of the evaluation as a process during which the understanding of the university was created through and in discourse of assessment. The assessment discourse helped to define the functional problems of the university, it supported the creation of managerial understanding of the university by focusing attention to irrational and unfunctional elements in the university structures (library, computer centre), and helped the faculties to see the problems in doctoral training more clearly than before. Finally, assessment discourse promoted the use of concepts shared by the participants of the total evaluation process.
>
> (Välimaa *et al.*, 1998: 31–2)

The authors go on to acknowledge that the university's different development documents and plans may tend to overstate the importance of an 'evaluative culture' in the university as a whole. They suggest that evaluation has been transformed into the administrative infrastructure. At the same time, they concede that evaluation has changed social relations within the university, giving rise to new social groupings concerned with curriculum structures, forms of tutoring and financing doctoral students, research priority areas and so on. However, like many other case-study authors, they emphasize the interaction of evaluation with other university processes and present an emerging university culture based on 'competition, political calculations, and strategic rhetorical game' (Välimaa *et al.*, 1998: 33), a culture which is supported but not defined by evaluation and assessment activity.

Conclusion

Despite some examples to the contrary, the impact of quality assessment upon university culture appears to have been to weaken subject-based culture at the level of the basic unit. It has done so by weakening group boundaries between departments and other units and by supporting the imposition of increasingly explicit values and regulations from the centre of the institution. These increasingly reflect external political and economic values and are part of a wider context of reduced funding, external competition and a growing emphasis upon the needs of consumers. External quality systems can in some circumstances support disciplinary cultures against such pressures, but more frequently they reinforce their effects.

The visibility of cultural change within universities differs between levels. It is most evident at the central level where the discourse of committees and planning documents responds to the requirements of outside pressures, including external quality assessment systems. The development of more managerial – and centralist – decision-making often appears to be necessary in order to promote new values and, in Maassen's words, 'ways of life', at potentially resistant faculty and departmental levels.

Cultural change appears to be generally less visible at the basic unit level. This might be expected in view of the fact that the existence of most basic units is still mainly defined in disciplinary terms. However, the weakening of basic unit or departmental boundaries appears to be reducing the power of the department over its individual staff members. Increasingly, academic staff belong to multiple groups – some defined in subject terms, others in functional terms such as access, technology, labour markets – and may acquire an individualistic mix of values and orientations from all of them. In institutions which have created and implemented far-reaching institution-wide policies and regulations, the cultural response at the level of individual staff members may be fatalism and compliance. In institutions where institutional policies are weak or ineffectively implemented, the resultant response from staff may be greater individualism. In either circumstance, there is some evidence from the case studies to suggest that individual staff members may be rather more responsive to the changing values embodied in quality assessment than are the basic departmental units to which they belong.

We end this chapter by repeating the caveat that the IMHE case studies are at their weakest in reporting impact at the basic unit or individual level. Other research (e.g. Bauer and Henkel, 1998) suggests that departmental cultures remain remarkably resistant to the kinds of changes described in this chapter and retain a powerful hold on the loyalties and values of most academic staff. As with so much else in contemporary higher education, the influence of quality management and quality assessment on academic cultures will depend on institutional and national contexts as well as differences between individual subjects.

Note

1. The factors determining student culture have been well described in the various studies by Becker *et al.* (1961, 1968) and more recently in Pascarella and Terenzini (1991).

10
Quality Assessment and Institutional Change

Introduction

The institutions which took part in the IMHE study were facing many problems: problems posed by features of the environment in which they were operating as well as those arising from the internal changes taking place at all levels. Was quality assessment seen as just one additional problem? Or was it regarded as a solution to some of their problems?

There was considerable diversity in the circumstances and experiences of the institutions which participated in the study. They represented different types of institutions, with different histories and ambitions, seeking to survive and prosper in different national contexts. Accordingly, few general statements about the institutions can be made. Perhaps the only one we can offer is that all of the participating institutions appeared to be making use of some form of quality assessment or evaluation as part of the management of institutional change. The role that external systems of quality assessment played varied but was not usually dominant.

In the first part of this final chapter, we will consider some of the ways in which institutions have used assessment and evaluation activities to help solve their current problems. We will review some of the developments which have taken place in institutions as a result of assessment activity – both internal and external – and consider how these relate to wider processes of change and decision-making in higher education.

In the second part, we will look at the specific contribution of external quality assessment systems, the role of national quality agencies and the part which they play in the mediation of relations between higher education institutions, the state and other interest groups.

The third part of the chapter will look again at the model for investigating the impact of quality assessment which we introduced in Chapter 2. We will consider the types of relationship between the elements of the model and the kinds of impact occurring as a result of quality assessment.

Quality management and assessment in the life of institutions

There was a lot of quality management and assessment activity in the case-study institutions. Much of it was directed from the centre, either in response to external accountability requirements or in order to stimulate internal changes. The need for internal change was usually stimulated by pressures from the external environment, of which the requirements of external quality assessment were but one factor. Other factors included cuts in levels of state funding, greater competition between institutions, and expansion of student numbers bringing in new types of student requiring new types of course. These factors differed in their importance between institutions and between countries, but no institutions were exempt from some combination of them. For elite research universities, it was essential to maintain a high reputation and to be equipped to succeed in increasingly global competion for students and research funds. For some small colleges, it was essential to acquire polytechnic or equivalent status within expanding and restructured higher education systems.

Virtually all institutions were facing new types of relationship with the state. Whatever the history of the institution along a control–autonomy continuum, it was likely to be facing multiple mechanisms of external control requiring greater levels of accountability. In some countries, this was accompanied by a more general growth of a culture of consumerism in which organizations of all kinds were expected to provide greater information to the public about their successes and failures, their strengths and weaknesses. This public information was liable to be used by the mass media to construct league tables and other forms of rankings of institutions.

Accordingly, institutions of mass higher education are being opened up to public scrutiny in ways unknown in previous decades. Within the academic community itself, in all but the smallest higher education systems, it is no longer possible to rely on private informal knowledge about institutions other than one's own: there are too many of them, and they are too diverse. Higher education is under pressure to provide some systematic information about itself and to make it publicly available.

With diversity comes hierarchy, formal and informal. Institutions must continuously work to maintain or improve their public standing and academic reputation. In a context where institutional successes receive public attention, it becomes possible for an institution to improve its reputation, to move up the 'league table'; but by the same token, movement in the opposite direction can also occur.

In a changing and volatile external environment, new forms of institutional management develop. Some of them may be purely financial: designed to ensure that the books continue to balance in a situation where external funding, whether from one or multiple sources, is insecure. But many of the managerial changes concern interpreting the external policy framework in terms of the threats and opportunities which it provides and attempting to position the institution to exploit the latter and to avoid the former. This implies institutional change and, probably, top-down institutional change. This is where the institutional level of decision-making can come into conflict with the infrastructure of the institution: the departments, institutes, research centres, or what we have tended to refer to as the basic units.

The pressures on institutions to change, described in earlier chapters, reflect external factors and extrinsic values. When governments expand their higher education systems, they usually have some extrinsic economic or social purpose in mind. Thus, funding for higher education is increasingly conditional – on achieving the purposes of the funder, whether for contract research, trained manpower, greater social equity or whatever. In order to survive and prosper, institutions must address these external purposes, and in typical cases must incorporate them into internal decision-making and, where necessary, modify established cultures.

All this is far removed from traditional conceptions of how institutions of higher education change. Change has been seen as gradual and bottom-up, responding to developments within academic disciplines, the growth of new knowledge, its classification and organization (Clark, 1983; Becher and Kogan, 1992; Maassen, 1998). Change is generated in the basic units and any external influences enter the institution at that level. In some subject fields (e.g. business and management), external influences are great; in others (e.g. history), they are minimal (Boys *et al.*, 1988).

In many countries it appears that no parts of higher education can any longer remain immune from external influences. Thus, the history professor is reminded that his or her student will have to get a job after graduating and that employers will expect graduates to have certain attributes relevant to their employment. The history professor may also be told that there are particular pedagogic techniques that should be adopted in order to develop these attributes. And from an entirely different part of the institution, the history professor may be informed of the number of research publications and external grants that will be needed in order to satisfy accountability requirements.

In many higher education institutions, processes of quality management are about achieving these sorts of changes. They are about ensuring that institutional values (the 'mission statement') permeate the whole of the institution. As such, quality management is as much about internal accountability and compliance as it is about improvement. This does not necessarily imply conflict between the centre and the basic units. For most higher education institutions, disciplinary excellence in teaching and research is the most highly prized value of all. But for many, it is a value that must be mediated by other factors, some of which we have set out above.

Quality management at the level of the institution appears to be about three main things. The first is the need to comply with whatever external quality demands are current in the national system. This comprises one of the main reasons why the institution will have set up a quality management system and why it takes a particular form. Depending on the national requirements, compliance will also entail the need to achieve assessment outcomes appropriate to the institution's self-perception and claimed status.

The second aspect of institutional quality management relates to the need to increase efficiency and effectiveness: to do better what the institution already does – to improve completion rates and student satisfaction on existing courses, to enhance research productivity, and to achieving these ends despite reduced resources.

The third aspect is to do with a change of institutional mission. This involves attempting to make the staff of the institution do different things: to make their courses more relevant to employment; to adopt new styles of teaching; to subordinate disciplinary priorities to thematic principles of course organization; to adopt semester systems; to undertake more applied research; to generate linkages with the local community; to teach in the evenings; to teach more often; and so on and so on. Depending on the national and the institutional context, some changes are modest, others dramatic.

Quality management systems at the institutional level were far from being the whole story of quality management and assessment in the IMHE case-study institutions: indeed, some had scarcely developed such systems. Yet within the infrastructure of these institutions, plenty of assessment and evaluation was going on. Some of it was in the form of ad hoc responses to problems such as falling enrolments or student complaints. A committee or working party would be set up to investigate the problem, to collect evidence and to make recommendations, usually to the parent departmental committee, designed to remove the problem. In some institutions, faculties had established traditions of periodic reviews of their teaching and research, often involving inputs from external academic peers. These reviews were not part of the requirements of some wider institutional system of quality management. They represented custom and practice within a particular faculty, a kind of academic 'stock-taking' linked to future planning and development.

Autonomous review procedures at faculty or departmental levels tended to be a feature of large research universities. Quality was the business of the faculty, not of the university. Institutional systems of accountability appeared often to be minimal, although if major problems arose the university leadership would usually find a way to intervene.

Many of the faculties and departments in the IMHE case-study institutions had recently experienced or were currently experiencing external reviews conducted by national quality agencies. Less was written in the case studies about these reviews than we had expected. In some institutions, they appeared to have been incorporated into whatever systems of institutional or faculty quality management already existed; in others, internal quality management procedures seemed to have been developed – or at least substantially modified – in order to fit into the requirements of the external system. In some countries institutions were subject to several forms of external requirement, for example state curriculum regulations and professional body requirements. Departments and faculties had to juggle these external requirements as well as attending to their own internal needs.

Some case-study authors wrote about the development of an 'evaluation culture' within their institutions. Insofar as a significant amount of time was being spent on evaluation and assessment activities, such a description might be warranted. However, it is not altogether clear how far the value and legitimacy of such activity was widely accepted within the institutions, or how far the results of these activities influenced decision-making. As we noted in Chapter 9, assessment and evaluation activities seemed to carry greater weight with the senior managers and committees of the institutions and with some individual teaching staff than they did with departments and faculties, where disciplinary interests and values apparently remained dominant.

The role of national agencies

In Europe at least, the emergence of national agencies charged with the assessment and assurance of quality has been one of the distinctive features of higher education during the 1990s. It is a development which has attracted much attention: in public debates about government policies, in academic conferences, in new specialist journals, in initiatives taken by international organizations such as the European Union, the Council of Europe and the Organization for Economic Co-operation and Development. This book has looked at some of the reasons for the creation of such agencies and at the impact of their work upon the institutions which collaborated in the IMHE study.

There appears to be an emerging orthodoxy, certainly in Europe, about the need for such organizations and the forms that they should take. In Chapter 5, we questioned how far the 'general model' promoted by the European Union and several of the established European quality agencies was really helpful in understanding external assessment and evaluation processes. It was not clear how far the model was meant to be descriptive of existing practice or prescriptive of future practice – and, if the latter, what the basis was for the prescriptiveness. If it was meant to be descriptive, we found problems applying each of the four elements to the countries which took part in the IMHE project.

The co-ordinating body sometimes did not exist; sometimes there were several of them; frequently the body seemed to do more than co-ordinate assessments, it actually carried them out. *Self-evaluation* seemed often to have no evaluative content, but merely to refer to the collection of descriptive data about the institution or programme as a basis for external scrutiny. *External peer review* posed significant questions for the interpretation of who constituted a 'peer'; we noted that not all agencies accepted or used the terminology. *Published reports* did however appear to be a common, if by no means universal, outcome of quality assessment although their content, style, length and intended audience could vary considerably.

If the model is intended to be prescriptive, many questions are posed for any country which decides to adopt it. Some of the most significant are: whether to focus at institutional or programme levels or both; what degree of authority and independence to give to 'peer review' groups; how to select them and whether to train them; whether to include summative judgements (perhaps in numerical form) as part of the assessment process; how to follow up the outcomes of assessment; who should do it; and what consequences should result?

Answers to these and other questions differ, reflecting the contextual features of higher education in different countries. The decision in each case should reflect the purposes of quality assessment although, as noted, these are not always clear. We observed that the practice of external quality assessment seemed often to be more to do with accountability than with improvement: accountability not only to the state, but to consumers and to the wider academic community. The need for accountability was generally accepted within institutions, at least at management levels.

In operational terms, the 'general model' seemed to be most applicable to medium-sized higher education systems with a tradition of state regulation. Small countries encountered practical difficulties in attempting to operate an objective and expert process of peer review in the absence of sufficiently large academic communities to provide objective peers. Large countries faced problems of achieving consistency and avoiding escalating costs in coping with the scale and complexity of mass and diverse higher education systems. While criteria of consistency and fairness called for the standardization of assessment procedures, criteria relating to diversity and 'fitness for purpose' called for more flexible procedures.

A tradition of state regulation seemed to ease the acceptance of external quality assessment within the academic community, in that it allowed a quid pro quo of relaxation of regulations in other areas. It also allowed more modest and achievable objectives to be set by governments for quality assessment, in the knowledge that it was but one element in a toolkit of control mechanisms. In countries without such a tradition, the introduction of quality assessment was more likely to be opposed as a matter of principle by the academic community, and more was expected of it by interventionist governments lacking other control mechanisms.

A further limitation to the 'general model' is that it tends to focus on only certain aspects of national quality management systems. Thus, much is written about the assessment system operated by the Association of Dutch Universities (Vereniging van Samenwerkende Nederlandse Universiteiten – VSNU) but relatively little about the role of the Inspectorate or the role of the state in regulating curricula and awards. Attention is rightly given to the long history of accreditation in the United States but rather less to state licensing or to national testing for entrance to graduate school. National testing has attracted interest in some Latin American countries, for example Brazil, as a direct way of addressing questions of comparability of standards in mass systems of higher education, but is ignored in the model.

External quality assessment systems seemed to interact with institutional quality management in three main ways. First, they were in some cases partly responsible for the creation of the institutional system and for shaping its form. This was likely to occur when the external system addressed issues at the institutional level and scrutinized internal decision-making procedures and accountability linkages between levels. It could also occur in cases where subject level assessment had public outcomes – for example, the UK grading system – which could damage the reputation of the institution as a whole. But all the case-study authors emphasized that the external quality system was only one factor among many which had influenced the development of quality management within their institutions.

Second, external quality assessment interacted with institutional quality management by providing it with information. In contrast to the sequence implied by the general model, where self-evaluation provides the basis for external evaluation, in practice it appeared that the results of external evaluation were being incorporated into internal quality management systems and were thereby contributing to institutional decision-making. Senior managers, in particular, tended to emphasize the value of an external view, both for its objectivity and its expert basis. Even where a national quality agency did not exist, institutions might bring in external peers – sometimes from other countries – to take part in internal reviews and other assessment activities. Where a quality agency did exist, its regular inputs into the institution's internal processes were frequently welcomed by managers, as were other external inputs from professional bodies, financial auditors, etc. This suggests that realistic institutional self-knowledge is not easy to achieve without external inputs and reference points.

The third way in which external and internal institutional quality systems could be seen to interact was in relation to the outcomes of individual assessments, particularly when these were negative. Again, contextual considerations needed to be taken into account. There were few if any cases reported where negative external assessments came out of the blue, but a number where known problems had not been acted upon for local reasons within an institution and where the external assessment provided the needed additional impetus for action to be taken. It has also to be said that there were some cases where known problems were not picked up by external assessment. When this happened, it made it more difficult to address the problems internally.

An important feature of quality agencies is the values which they represent. As a potential route through which extrinsic values and interests can enter higher education institutions, they can act as an important source of change, challenging cultures based on disciplinary values and interests. In Chapter 2, we suggested that there were four broad types of values that could inform quality management and assessment. The first of these we termed 'academic', their source being the cultures of academic disciplines. In their context, conceptions of quality would differ across the various basic units of an institution's infrastructure. The second type of value we referred to as 'managerial', deriving from the procedures and mechanisms of the institution for ensuring the quality of its activities. These would tend to be invariant across the institution, setting limits to the autonomy of basic units and the extent to which disciplinary values and interests were able to prevail. The third type of value we termed 'pedagogic', again invariant across the institution. The source of quality in this type is the technical – rather than the disciplinary – proficiency in teaching skills of academic staff. The final type we described as 'employment-related' – consumerist would be an alternative description – where employment requirements constitute the source of values. In this type, the emphasis would be upon the outcomes of education, the skills and competences of graduates and their relevance to employment needs. Research tends to be more clearly either 'academic' or 'consumerist' in its value orientations. The full range applies mainly to the teaching or educational functions of higher education.

Chapter 9 referred to cultural changes in the direction of a growth of managerialism at the institutional level and support for a greater emphasis upon teaching among individual academic staff. These were general trends rather than the direct effects of external quality assessment. With regard to how far external quality assessment systems appear to be changing the value orientations of higher education institutions, conclusions must be tentative. From the IMHE case studies, a complex picture emerges.

A majority of the national quality assessment agencies included in this study used, as their main methodology, external review at subject or programme level. Review was primarily peer review and peers were primarily subject experts. Thus, assessment might be expected to take place within the culture and values of the discipline and do nothing to undermine them. Indeed, in a few institutions where the mission and internal organization of the institution emphasized interdisciplinarity and consumerist values, external assessment served to strengthen academic values and disciplinary culture. Thus, to an important extent, external quality assessment as practised in many of the countries which took part in the IMHE study was a source of protection of intrinsic academic values against a variety of external and internal pressures.

This, however, was not the complete picture. Agencies differed in the extent to which they allowed academic values to dominate quality assessment. In most systems, employer interests were given recognition in the assessment process where appropriate (and there were wide differences in what was considered appropriate). Pedagogic experts, students, representatives of professional bodies, as well as employers, frequently took part in review teams, thus raising questions about the appropriateness of the term 'peer review'. And there were other ways in which agencies could limit the power of disciplinary values. The specification of guidelines and criteria of assessment could give weight to factors outside of disciplinary concerns. Training of subject peers in the use of such guidelines could reinforce the agency's conception of quality over that held within the disciplines.

There was another subtle way in which the importance of disciplinary values could be lessened in the assessment process. This was apparent from the study which we undertook of the impact of the quality assessment process in England (Brennan, Frederiks and Shah, 1997). Several academic staff who were interviewed for that project indicated a preference for assessment to focus on pedagogic or procedural issues. This was because the purpose of the assessment was perceived to be mainly summative. In this context, assessment of disciplinary competence – for example, through scrutiny of curriculum choices, reading lists, etc – was too close to the central tenets of the academic self-conception to be welcomed with equanimity. This was particularly true of staff in the more elite research universities who tended to question the competence of the external peers to make judgements about disciplinary matters. Criticism of one's teaching or administrative proficiency was one thing; the possibility of criticism of one's disciplinary expertise was much more threatening. All involved in the peer review process preferred to avoid entering into curriculum and disciplinary debate. However, a more developmental focus to the assessment process – formative rather than summative evaluation – might well have produced a rather different reaction. There was some evidence that this would have been welcomed, albeit in the less elite institutions (Brennan, Frederiks and Shah, 1997).

If the predominance of disciplinary values in the external peer review process can be limited by the actions of national agencies, they can be further limited by the actions of institutional managers and administrators. Whether institutions intervene in the preparatory stages of external assessment of basic units or whether they use the results of such assessments for internal decision-making purposes, the effects are to lessen the disciplinary-specific context of the assessment and to strengthen the managerial context. Institutional intervention must nearly always reflect values extrinsic to individual disciplines, the principal exception being in specialist or monotechnic institutions where disciplinary values are shared across the whole organization.

External quality assessment is not always directed at the subject level. Institutional-level assessment is almost wholly managerial in focus, whether it is examining institutional quality management and decision-making procedures (UK quality audit), legal and financial matters (US institutional accreditation), or compliance with state regulations (accreditation in some central and eastern European countries).

As we have noted – and as many of the IMHE case studies have emphasized – institutional quality management systems tend to reflect values which are invariant across the institution: managerial generally, pedagogic and consumerist sometimes, depending upon the mission and type of institution. This is not because institutions do not value disciplinary values and excellence: usually quite the reverse. But because these values are to a large degree the private property of academic basic units, it is difficult for the institution to incorporate them in its own systems and procedures. This is why external quality assessment at subject level is so valuable, if done well. In some countries (e.g. France), institutional and subject-level assessments have been bound together into a single – although extended – process. This seems particularly to strengthen central institutional authority (traditionally weak in France) as the results of individual assessments are mediated through the whole institution's context of assessment.[1]

The impact of quality assessment

Our model for investigating the impact of quality assessment distinguished between impact through rewards, through changing institutional policies and structures, and through changing cultures. We further argued that the nature of the impact was a function of the methods used and the national and institutional context of the assessment.

With the important exception of the case studies of the two Mexican universities, impacts through rewards occurred as a result of external rather than internal assessment. Although direct financial rewards were rather rare, rewards in terms of reputation, influence and status allocation were quite common. They were more likely to occur when assessments included a clear summative, preferably quantifiable, judgement. Linkages of assessment to rewards seemed to find acceptance among those whom the quality assessment process affected (positively or negatively). If rewards were going to take place anyway – reflecting increasing system and institutional differentiation – then it was preferable that their recipients should be identified on the basis of quality assessment results rather than on political grounds. Rewards could occur at all levels, from the salaries of individual academic staff in Mexico to the status designation of a whole institution in Finland. Some types of reward (e.g. financial) could take immediate effect; others (e.g. reputational) were likely to be more long term.

The impact of quality assessment through changing institutional policies and structures was seen to be a complex process. External quality assessment, particularly when focused at the institutional level, tended to be associated with the development of institution-wide quality management policies and procedures. Such institutional policies were frequently part of much wider processes of centralization and managerialism. A wide range of external factors, including increased accountability and greater competition, were giving rise to these changes within institutions. External quality assessment appeared not to be a principal cause. Indeed, when quality assessment operated at the subject level, there was – as noted earlier – some indication that it could strengthen disciplinary and departmental interests within the structure of the institution.

The introduction of institution-wide quality management policies was frequently associated with, without causing, fundamental organizational and decision-making changes. They were often integrated into planning processes within the institution, as part of the creation of a corporate approach to institutional management, contributing to the internal processes of accountability and to the introduction of line-management in place of collegiate decision-making structures. Where the fundamental changes of this kind were being introduced they appeared to affect all areas of institutional decision-making.

In contrast, external quality assessments, insofar as they impacted directly on institutional policies and structures, did so in quite limited and specific ways: for example on library policy, on curriculum structures in a particular subject field, or on methods of student feedback. That is to say, the changes directly provoked by external quality assessment were specific and substantive rather than fundamental. The indirect changes resulting from quality assessment were potentially more wide-ranging but were difficult to measure.

The impact of quality assessment through changes in institutional cultures manifested itself in two main ways. One, related to changing institutional structures and policies, was in the promotion of a managerial ethos across institutions – an ethos that worked to replace the informal with the formal, the implicit with the explicit, the disciplinary culture with an enterprise culture. The second was in terms of attitudes to teaching. In the case-study institutions, more time than in the past was devoted to discussing teaching, to monitoring it, to seeking ways to improve it. Changes to teaching attitudes were often resisted at basic unit levels where they were seen to challenge disciplinary authority and values. They were likely to be promoted from the institutional centre and embraced by a few individual teachers but resisted more widely in departments, particularly in certain disciplines. These tendencies were balanced in many institutions by the effects of self-evaluation activities which strengthened collective behaviour and attitudes at basic unit levels, often reinforcing disciplinary cultures.

As we have noted earlier in this chapter, external quality assessment is a route through which institutional cultures are opened up to extrinsic interests. However, at least on the surface, academic values prevail in the external systems of peer review operated by most of the national quality agencies. Beneath the surface may lie other values, introduced into the quality assessment process through agency guidelines, training and the extension of the concept of 'peer' to include wider interest groups.

Conclusion

Debate about higher education has been described as being between protagonists of 'elite nostalgia' on the one hand and of 'mass modernization' on the other (Parker and Courtney, 1998). We began this book with the suggestion that the notion of quality in higher education tended to arouse enthusiasm and cynicism in equal measure. There may be a relationship between the two sets of attitudes, with the enthusiasts for quality management being firmly on the side of the mass modernisers and the cynics in support of elite nostalgia.

As we have indicated throughout this book, there is a strong relationship between quality management and assessment and the expansion and diversification of higher education. The latter developments have required changes within higher education institutions and have brought increased pressures for the greater accountability of the higher education system to the rest of society.

In practice, we have seen in the IMHE case studies many examples of institutional managers using quality assessment as a tool in the wider process of managing organizational change. But we have also seen examples of actions by groups of academic staff taken as part of quality assessment processes which have been about preserving and indeed strengthening quite traditional discipline-based conceptions of academic quality. In the lives of the institutions in the IMHE study, external quality assessment and the agencies which supported it were essentially 'noises off stage': occasionally a nuisance, sometimes threatening, now and then quite useful but, on the whole, a fact of life in an increasingly complex external environment. This is not to imply that external quality assessment has failed to make any impact upon higher education institutions. Virtually all of the case-study institutions were able to report changes which had occurred, at least indirectly, as a result of quality assessment. It was simply that there were larger external forces acting on higher education. In different contexts, quality assessment might act as a conduit to these larger forces or as a source of resistance to them.

Inevitably, the IMHE case studies tended to be written by enthusiasts rather than cynics. After all, why would the cynics bother? So it must be acknowledged that the case studies provide a biased perspective, albeit a rich and varied one. Where possible, we have referred to other studies which have looked at the impact of assessment from different perspectives. But there remain few such studies which report on the impact of quality assessment through the eyes of ordinary academic staff, still less from the perspectives of students. There would be value in linking the emerging literature on the methods and effects of quality assessment to the more established literature on the effects of higher education on students and on the factors which appear to influence learning.

One of us concluded an earlier article based on this study in an essentially optimistic tone:

> quality is taking up a lot of time. Across the world academics are busy assessing each other. And it is surely through this industry of reciprocal 'visiting' that small, scarcely visible, incremental changes are being encouraged. Quality assessment invites us to cross boundaries, to construct new bridges between institutions and between basic units of institutions . . .
>
> (Brennan, 1997: 23–4)

Now, three years on, we want to modify the emphasis of this conclusion, although without losing the optimistic tone. Changes in many higher education institutions are today highly visible. They verge on the revolutionary rather than the incremental. There is surely a need to understand them better and, if need be, to control them more carefully. Quality management and assessment processes can help us to do this, but only if we are open and critical about their purposes, methods and effects. At its most effective, quality assessment is about learning and about sharing the lessons of that learning. It is about crossing boundaries, about constructing bridges, about confronting vested interests, about accepting change as seen through critical and sometimes sceptical eyes.

Closure of the debate about quality assessment is premature. Many of its effects are likely to be long term and most are heavily contingent on other factors affecting higher education. Although we are well aware of the widespread demands for simple models and methods of quality assessment, we hope that such demands will be resisted. Quality assessment is a complex business.

Note

1. Personal communication from the Secretary General, Comité National d'Évaluation.

Appendix I: Institutional Case Studies

The following case studies were prepared by institutions for the project. They represent a snapshot of what was happening in the institutions between 1995 and 1997.

Australia

Monash University*
University of Newcastle
University of Western Sydney, Nepean

Belgium

The Catholic University in Leuven
The Free University of Brussels

Canada

The CEGEP [Collège d'Enseignement Général et Professionel] Saint Jérome

Denmark

University of Aalborg*

Finland

University of Helsinki
University of Jyväskylä
University of Oulu
Vantaa Polytechnic

France

Louis Pasteur University, Strasbourg
University of Lille III – Charles de Gaulle
University of the Social Sciences, Toulouse I

Greece

Athens University of Economics and Business
The Technological and Educational Institute of Patras

Hungary

Bessenyei Teacher Training College (Nyregyhaza)
Kolcsey Teacher Training College (Debrecen)

Italy

The University of Venice

Mexico

Autonomous Metropolitan University, Mexico City
Autonomous National University of Mexico

The Netherlands

The University of Amsterdam
The University of Maastricht
The Technical University, Delft

Spain

The Polytechnic University of Catalunya

Sweden

University of Uppsala*

United Kingdom

Cardiff University of Wales
The Open University
Sheffield Hallam University

Note: All the case studies, except the three marked with an asterisk, have been published on the IMHE website (http://www.oecd.org/els/edu/imhe). The case studies of the universities of Aalborg, Monash and Uppsala have been published in Brennan, J., deVries, P. and Williams, R. (eds) (1997) *Standards and Quality in Higher Education*. London: Jessica Kingsley.

In addition to the institutional case studies, the following national quality assessment agencies prepared case studies which reported on their perspectives of the effects they have had on their respective higher education institutions. These have not been published.

The Association of Dutch Universities (VSNU), The Netherlands
Centre for Quality Assurance and Evaluation, Denmark
National Evaluation Committee, France

Foundation of Portuguese Universities/Council of Rectors, Portugal
Institution for Studies in Research and Higher Education, Norway
Evaluation Agency, Lower Saxony, Germany
Council of Universities, Spain

Appendix II: Framework for Institutional Case Studies

1 Purpose

1.1 The purpose of this framework document was to provide guidance to case-study authors as to focus and content and to facilitate synthesis and comparability for the final report of the project. It was not meant to be prescriptive and authors were encouraged to draw out possibly unique features of their own institutional experiences.

2 Focus of the case studies

2.1 The case studies focused on the following:

(a) the *contexts* for quality assessment: e.g. national system features, government policies towards HE (including main forms of state regulation), external quality assessment requirements, institutional characteristics

(b) the *internal quality assurance methods* that are in place within the institution, for example self-evaluation, use of external examiners, student feedback, regular review and monitoring of courses and departments, staff appointment procedures, etc

(c) how quality assurance (both internal and external) affects the *management and decision-making processes*: e.g. relationship to planning and resourcing, curriculum development, incentives etc at different levels within the institution

(d) the *impacts* of external quality requirements upon the institution at structural, cultural, curriculum and governance levels. Institutions were asked to give specific examples, e.g. establishment of new committees, appointment of new managers, changing role of professors, deployment of resources, staff development practices, approaches to teaching and learning

(e) where possible, institutions undertook internal *case studies* (within the overall institutional case study) of recently evaluated departments or disciplines in order particularly to compare the impact of both positive and negative evaluations

(f) the *interpretation* of outcomes from the quality assessments and how the *future* of an institution's mission, policies, structure and culture related to this.

Authors were asked to address all of the above in the context of institutional and system change.

2.2   Examples of some of the issues which case-study authors were asked to address were the following:

- how quality assessment enters into the management and decision-making process
- the impact on governance
- the impacts on institutional management generally
- the impacts upon the nature of academic work and the distribution of academic and administrative staff time
- the relationship between quality assurance systems and educational outcomes
- the validity of assessment
- where the aim of the quality assessment process is improvement/enhancement, does it work?
- the relationship between accountability, value for money and quality improvement
- are there any incentive structures for staff?
- the impact on institutional mission overall
- the impact on the student experience of HE
- the extent to which quality assessment takes account of external influences, e.g. labour markets.

Appendix III: Framework for Case Studies of Impact by National Quality Assurance Agencies

1   Purpose

1.1   This framework document provided guidance to agency case-study authors as to focus and content and to facilitate synthesis and comparability for the final report of the project. It was not meant to be prescriptive and authors were encouraged to draw out possibly unique features of their own agency experiences.

2   Sources of information about impact

Please indicate the main sources of information about the impact of external quality assessment available to the agency – e.g. systematic follow-up of recommendations, informal feed-back, agency-commissioned studies, independent studies.

3   Focus of the case studies

3.1   (a) the *contexts* for quality assessment: e.g. system features, government policies towards HE (including main forms of state regulation), external quality assessment requirements, institutional characteristics

       (b) main *audiences* for quality assessment, e.g. institutional managers, academic staff, government, students, employers etc, forms and distribution of reports

       (c) the extent to which typical *internal quality assurance methods* that are in place within institutions (e.g. self-evaluation, use of external examiners, student feedback, regular review and monitoring of courses and departments, staff appointment procedures, etc) meet external QA requirements and the extent to which they need to be adapted to meet external requirements

       (d) where applicable, agency perceptions of how quality assurance (both internal and external) affects the *management and decision-making processes*: e.g. relationship to planning and resourcing, curriculum development, incentives etc at different levels within the institution

       (e) where applicable, agency perceptions of the *impacts* of external quality requirements upon institutions at structural, cultural, curriculum and governance levels, e.g. establishment of new committees, appointment of new managers, changing role of professors, deployment of resources, staff development practices, approaches to teaching and learning

(f) *system-wide outcomes*, e.g. creation of new networks, exchange of information, changing balance between teaching, research and administration, altered reputations of institutions

(g) *political and social support*, e.g. greater political support/funding for HE, changing student preferences for courses/institutions, altered public perceptions about HE as a whole and about individual institutions.

Authors were asked to address all of the above in the context of institutional and system change.

3.2 Examples of some of the issues which the case-study authors were asked to address were the following:

- how quality assessment enters into the management and decision-making process
- the impact on governance
- the impacts on institutional management generally
- the impacts upon the nature of academic work and the distribution of academic and administrative staff time
- the relationship between quality assurance systems and educational outcomes
- the validity of assessment
- where the aim of the quality assessment process is improvement/enhancement, does it work?
- the relationship between accountability, value for money and quality improvement
- are there any incentive structures for staff?
- the impact on institutional mission overall
- the impact on the student experience of HE
- the extent to which quality assessment takes account of external influences, e.g. labour markets
- responsiveness of institutions at various levels, i.e. extent of willingness or compliance in relation to external requirements/recommendations.

References

Adonis, A. and Pollard, S. (1997) *A Class Act: The Myth of Britain's Classless Society*. London: Hamish Hamilton.

Antikainen, E.L. and Mattila, P. (1998) Case Study of Vantaa Polytechnic, http://www.oecd.org/els/edu/imhe

Arnold, G. (1998) Case Study of Sheffield Hallam University, http://www.oecd.org/els/edu/imhe

Baldwin, G. (1997) An Australian approach to quality in higher education: the case of Monash University, in J. Brennan, P. de Vries and R. Williams (eds) *Standards and Quality in Higher Education*. London: Jessica Kingsley.

Barblan, A. (1997) Management for quality: the CRE programme of institutional evaluation: issues encountered in the pilot phase – 1994/5, in J. Brennan, P. de Vries and R. Williams (eds) *Standards and Quality in Higher Education*. London: Jessica Kingsley.

Barnett, R. (1992) *Improving Higher Education: Total Quality Care*. Buckingham: SRHE and Open University Press.

Barnett, R. (1994) Power, enlightenment and quality evaluation, *European Journal of Education*, 29(2): 165–79.

Bauer, M. and Henkel, M. (1998) Academic responses to quality reforms in higher education, in M. Henkel and B. Little (eds) *Changing Relationships between Higher Education and the State*. London: Jessica Kingsley.

Becher, T. (1989) *Academic Tribes and Territories: Intellectual Enquiry and the Cultures of Disciplines*. Buckingham: SRHE and Open University Press.

Becher, T. and Kogan, M. (1992) *Process and Structure in Higher Education*, second edition. London: Routledge.

Becker, H., Geer, B., Hughes, E. and Strauss, A. (1961) *Boys in White: Student Culture in Medical School*. Chicago: University of Chicago Press.

Becker, H., Geer, B. and Hughes, E. (1968) *Making the Grade: The Academic Side of College Life*. New York: Wiley.

Bellefroid, F. and Elen, J. (1998) Case Study of the University of Leuven, http://www.oecd.org/els/edu/imhe

Berger, P. (1966) *Invitation to Sociology*. London: Penguin.

Biglan, A. (1973) The characteristics of subject matter in different academic areas; and Relationships between subject matter characteristics and the structure and output of university departments, *Journal of Applied Psychology*, 57(3): 195–213.

Bodson, S. (1998) Case Study of the Free University of Brussels,
http://www.oecd.org/els/edu/imhe
Bourdieu, P. (1996) *The State Nobility: Elite Schools in the Field of Power*. Cambridge: Polity Press.
Boys, C., Brennan, J., Henkel, M., Kirkland, J., Kogan, M. and Youll, P. (1988) *Higher Education and the Preparation for Work*. London: Jessica Kingsley.
Brennan, J. (1997) Authority, legitimacy and change: the rise of quality assessment in higher education, *Higher Education Management*, 9(1): 7–30.
Brennan, J., Lyon, E.S., McGeevor, P.A. and Murray, K. (1993) *Students, Courses and Jobs: The Relationship between Higher Education and the Labour Market*. London: Jessica Kingsley.
Brennan, J., El-Khawas, E. and Shah, T. (1994) *Peer Review and the Assessment of Higher Education Quality: An International Perspective*. London: QSC/OU.
Brennan, J., Shah, T. and Williams, R. (1996) *Quality Assessment and Quality Improvement: An Analysis of the Recommendations Made by the HEFCE Assessors*. Bristol: HEFCE/QSC.
Brennan, J., deVries, P. and Williams, R. (eds) (1997) *Standards and Quality in Higher Education*. London: Jessica Kingsley.
Brennan, J., Frederiks, M. and Shah, T. (1997) *Improving the Quality of Education: The Impact of Quality Assessment on Institutions*. London: HEFCE/QSC.
Brennan, J., Holloway, J. and Shah, T. (1998) Case Study of the UK Open University,
http://www.oecd.org/els/edu/imhe
Cheminat, A. and Hoffert, M. (1998) Case Study of the University of Strasbourg,
http://www.oecd.org/els/edu/imhe
Clark, B.R. (1970) *The Distinctive College: Antiochy, Reed, Swarthmore*. Chicago: Aldine.
Clark, B.R. (1972) The organisational saga in higher education, *Administrative Science Quarterly*, 17: 178–84.
Clark, B.R. (1983) *The Higher Education System: Academic Organisation in Cross-National Perspective*. Berkeley: University of California Press.
Clark, B.R. (1998) *Creating Entrepreneurial Universities: Organisational Pathways of Transformation*. Oxford: Pergamon.
Cohen, M.D. and March, J.G. (1974) *Leadership and Ambiguity: The American College President*. New York: McGraw Hill.
Collins, R. (1975) *Conflict Sociology: Toward an Explanatory Science*. New York: Academic Press.
Cowen, R. (ed.) (1996) *The Evaluation of Higher Education Systems*. London: Kogan Page.
Daniels, C. (1998) Case Study of Cardiff University of Wales,
http://www.oecd.org/els/edu/imhe
de Klerk, R., Visser, K. and van Welie, L. (1998) Case Study of the University of Amsterdam,
http://www.oecd.org/els/edu/imhe
deVries, P. (1996) Could 'criteria' used in quality assessment be classified as academic standards?, *Higher Education Quarterly*, 50(3): 193–206.
Dill, D. (1995) Through Deming's eyes: a cross-national analysis of quality assurance policies in higher education, *Quality in Higher Education*, 1(2): 95–110.
Dill, D. (1997) Accreditation, assessment, anarchy? The evolution of academic quality assurance policies in the United States, in J. Brennan, P. de Vries and R. Williams (eds) *Standards and Quality in Higher Education*. London: Jessica Kingsley.
Douglas, M. (1982) *In the Active Voice*. London: Routledge and Kegan Paul.
Douglas, M. (1986) *How Institutions Think*. Syracuse, New York: Syracuse University Press.
EC PHARE and European Training Foundation (1998a) *Quality Assurance in Higher Education: A Legislative Review and Needs Analysis of Developments in Central and Eastern Europe*. Turin: European Training Foundation.
EC PHARE and European Training Foundation (1998b) *Quality Assurance in Higher Education: Final Report and Project Recommendations*. London: QSC/OU.

El-Khawas, E. (1998) 'Higher education research, policy and practice: patterns of communication and miscommunication', paper presented at the International Symposium on the Institutional Basis of Higher Education Research: Experiences and Perspectives, 1–2 September 1998. Kassel, Germany.

Engwall, L. (1997) A Swedish approach to quality in higher education: the case of Uppsala University, in J. Brennan, P. de Vries and R. Williams (eds) *Standards and Quality in Higher Education*. London: Jessica Kingsley.

European Commission (1995) *Initiatives of Quality Assurance and Assessment of Higher Education in Europe*. Luxembourg: Office for Official Publications of the European Communities.

European Commission (1997) *European Co-operation in Quality Assurance in Higher Education*, COM(97). Luxembourg: Office for Official Publications of the European Communities.

European Commission (1998) Recommendation of the Council of September 24, 1998 on European co-operation in quality assurance in higher education, *Official Journal of European Communities* (OJEC), L270. Luxembourg: Office for Official Publications of the European Commission.

Filep, L. (1998) Case Study of the Teacher Training College of Nyiregyhaza, http://www.oecd.org/els/edu/imhe

Finch, J. (1997) Power, legitimacy and academic standards, in J. Brennan, P. de Vries and R. Williams (eds) *Standards and Quality in Higher Education*. London: Jessica Kingsley.

Frazer, M. (1997) Report of the modalities of external evaluation of higher education in Europe: 1995–1997, *Higher Education in Europe*, 22(3): 349–401.

Frederiks, M., Westerheijden, D.F. and Weusthof, P. (1994) Effects of quality assessment in Dutch higher education, *European Journal of Education*, 29: 101–18.

Gellert, C. (1998) *European Higher Education Systems*. London: Jessica Kingsley.

Goedegebuure, L., Kaiser, F., Maassen, P., Meek, L., van Vught, F. and de Weert, E. (1993) *Higher Education Policy: An International and Comparative Perspective*. Oxford: Pergamon Press.

Harvey, L. and Green, D. (1993) Defining quality, *Assessment and Evaluation in Higher Education*, 18(1): 9–34.

Henkel, M. (forthcoming) *Academic Identities and Policy Change*. London: Jessica Kingsley.

Higher Education Funding Council for England (1997) *Fund for the Development of Teaching and Learning (FDTL) Phase One: HEFCE and DENI Awards*. Bristol: HEFCE.

Hofstede, G. (1991) *Cultures and Organisations: Software of the Mind*. London, New York: McGraw Hill.

Hyvärinen, K., Hämäläinen, K. and Pakkanen, P. (1998) Case Study of the University of Helsinki, http://www.oecd.org/els/edu/imhe

Kells, H.R. (1988) *Self-Study Processes: A Guide for Postsecondary and Similar Service-Oriented Institutions and Programs*, third edition. New York: ACE/Macmillan.

Kells, H.R. (1992) *Self Regulation in Higher Education: A Multinational Perspective on Collaborative Systems of Quality Assurance and Control*. London: Jessica Kingsley.

Kells, H.R. (1993) *The Development of Performance Indicators for Higher Education: A Compendium for Eleven Countries*. Paris: OECD/IMHE.

Kells, H.R. (1995) Creating a culture of evaluation and self regulation in higher education organisations, *Total Quality Management*, 6(5–6): 457–67.

Kells, H.R. (1998) 'National evaluation systems: propositions and lessons for the research and policy void', paper presented at the 11th Annual Conference of the Consortium of Higher Education Researchers, 3–5 September 1998. Kassel: Germany.

Kelsall, K., Kuhn, A. and Poole, A. (1970) *Graduates: The Sociology of an Elite*. London: Routledge.

Kerr, C. (1982) *The Uses of the University*. Cambridge, Mass.: Harvard University Press.

Kogan, M. (1986) *Educational Accountability: An Analytical Overview*. London: Hutchinson.

Kogan, M. and Kogan, P. (1984) *Higher Education Under Attack*. London: Kogan Page.

Kogan, M. and Hanney, S. (1999) *Reforming Higher Education*. London: Jessica Kingsley.

Lester, K. (1998) Case Study of the University of Newcastle, http://www.oecd.org/els/edu/imhe

Liuhanen, A., Sippola, P. and Karjalainen, A. (1998) Case Study of the University of Oulu, http://www.oecd.org/els/edu/imhe

Losfeld, G. and Verin, A. (1998) Case Study of the Charles de Gaulle University, Lille III, http://www.oecd.org/els/edu/imhe

Maassen, P. (1996) *Governmental Steering and the Academic Culture: The Intangibility of the Human Factor in Dutch and German Universities*. Maarsen: De Tijdstroom.

Maassen, P.A.M. and Westerheijden, D.F. (1998) Following the follow-up: a sketch of evaluation use in European higher education, in J.P. Scheele, P.A.M. Maassen and D.F. Westerheijden (eds) *To Be Continued . . . Follow-up of Quality Assurance in Higher Education*. Maarsen: Elsevier/De Tijdstroom.

Massaro, V. (1997) Institutional responses to quality assessment in Australia, in J. Brennan, P. de Vries and R. Williams (eds) *Standards and Quality in Higher Education*. London: Jessica Kingsley.

Mikol, M. (1998) Case Study of the University of Western Sydney, Nepean, http://www.oecd.org/els/edu/imhe

Neave, G. (1988) On the cultivation of quality efficiency and enterprise: an overview of recent trends in higher education in Western Europe, 1986–88, *European Journal of Education*, 23(1–2): 7–23.

Neave, G. and van Vught, F. (eds) (1991) *Prometheus Bound: The Changing Relationship between Government and Higher Education in Western Europe*. Oxford: Pergamon Press.

Parker, M. and Courtney, J. (1998) Universities or nurseries? Education, professionals and taxpayers, in D. Jary and M. Parker (eds) *The New Higher Education: Issues and Directions for the Post-Dearing University*. Stoke-on-Trent: Staffordshire University Press.

Pascarella, E.T. and Terenzini, P.T. (1991) *How College Affects Students: Findings and Insights from Twenty Years of Research*. San Francisco: Jossey-Bass.

Quality Assurance Agency for Higher Education (1998) *Quality Assurance: A New Approach*. Gloucester: QAA.

Rasmussen, P. (1997) A Danish approach to quality in higher education: the case of Aalborg University, in J. Brennan, P. de Vries and R. Williams (eds) *Standards and Quality in Higher Education*. London: Jessica Kingsley.

Reuke, H. (1997) *Quality Management, Quality Assessment and the Decision-Making Process in Lower Saxony, Germany*. The Evaluation Agency.

Rojo, L., Seco. R., Martinez, M. and Malo, S. (1998) Case Study of Universidad Nacional Autónoma de Mexico, http://www.oecd.org/els/edu/imhe

Saint-Girons, B. and Vincens, J.M. (1998) Case Study of Université des Sciences Sociales, Toulouse I, http://www.oecd.org/els/edu/imhe

Salter, B. and Tapper, T. (1994) *The State and Higher Education*. London: Woburn Press.

Scott, P. (1995) *The Meanings of Mass Higher Education*. Buckingham: SRHE and Open University Press.

Taylor, L. (1994) Reflecting on teaching: the benefits of self-evaluation, *Assessment and Evaluation in Higher Education*, 19(2): 109–122.

Thune, C. (1994) Setting up the Danish Centre, in A. Craft (ed.) *International Developments in Assuring Quality in Higher Education*. London: Falmer Press.

Thune, C. (1997) The Balance Between Accountability and Improvement: The Danish Experience, in J. Brennan, P. de Vries and R. Williams (eds) *Standards and Quality in Higher Education*. London: Jessica Kingsley.

Thune, C. and Staropoli, A. (1997) The European pilot project for evaluating quality in higher education, in J. Brennan, P. de Vries and R. Williams (eds) *Standards and Quality in Higher Education*. London: Jessica Kingsley.

Trow, M. (1994a) *Academic Reviews and the Culture of Excellence*. Stockholm: The Council for Studies of Higher Education.

Trow, M. (1994b) *Managerialism and the Academic Profession: Quality and Control*. London: QSC/Open University.

Trow, M. (1996) 'On the accountability of higher education in the United States', paper presented at the Princeton Conference on Higher Education, March.

Valenti, G. and Varela, G. (1998) Case Study of Universidad Autónoma Metropolitana Mexico, http://www.oecd.org/els/edu/imhe

Välimaa, J., Aittola, T. and Konttinnen, R. (1998) Case Study of the University of Jyvaskyla, http://www.oecd.org/els/edu/imhe

van Vught, F. (1994) Intrinsic and extrinsic aspects of quality assessment in higher education, in D.F. Westerheijden, J. Brennan and P.A.M. Maassen (eds) *Changing Contexts of Quality Assessment: Recent Trends in West European Higher Education*. Utrecht: LEMMA.

van Vught, F. and Westerheijden, D.F. (1993) *Quality Management and Quality Assurance in European Higher Education: Methods and Mechanisms*. Luxembourg: Office of the Official Publications of the European Commission.

Vroeijenstijn, A.I. (1994) Preparing for the second cycle, in D.F. Westerheijden, J. Brennan and P.A.M. Maassen (eds) *Changing Contexts of Quality Assessment: Recent Trends in West European Higher Education*. Utrecht: LEMMA.

Vroeijenstijn, A.I. (1995) *Improvement and Accountability: Navigating between Scylla and Charybdis*. London: Jessica Kingsley.

Warglein, M. and Savoia, M. (1998) Case Study of the Università Ca' Foscari di Venezia, Italy, http://www.oecd.org/els/edu/imhe

Watson, D. (1997) Quality, standards and institutional reciprocity, in J. Brennan, P. de Vries and R. Williams (eds) *Standards and Quality in Higher Education*. London: Jessica Kingsley.

Westerheijden, D.F. (1990) Peers, performance and power: quality assessment in the Netherlands, in L.D.J. Goedegebuure, P.A.M. Maassen and D.F. Westerheijden (eds) *Peer Review and Performance Indicators: Quality Assessment in British and Dutch Higher Education*. Utrecht: LEMMA.

Whitty, G., Power, S., Edwards, T. and Wigfall, V. (1998) *Destined for Success? Educational Biographies of Academically Able Pupils*. Report of a project funded by the Economic and Social Research Council. London: Institute of Education, University of London.

Zijderveld, D.C. (1997) Case Study of Impact by a National Quality Assurance Agency: The Case of the Netherlands. Unpublished. VSNU.

Index

The Society for Research into Higher Education

The Society for Research into Higher Education (SRHE) exists to stimulate and co-ordinate research into all aspects of higher education. It aims to improve the quality of higher education through the encouragement of debate and publication on issues of policy, on the organization and management of higher education institutions, and on the curriculum, teaching and learning methods.

The Society is entirely independent and receives no subsidies, although individual events often receive sponsorship from business or industry. The Society is financed through corporate and individual subscriptions and has members from many parts of the world.

Under the imprint *SRHE & Open University Press*, the Society is a specialist publisher of research, having over 80 titles in print. In addition to *SRHE News*, the Society's newsletter, the Society publishes three journals: *Studies in Higher Education* (three issues a year), *Higher Education Quarterly* and *Research into Higher Education Abstracts* (three issues a year).

The Society runs frequent conferences, consultations, seminars and other events. The annual conference in December is organized at and with a higher education institution. There are a growing number of networks which focus on particular areas of interest, including:

Access	Learning Environment
Assessment	Legal Education
Consultants	Managing Innovation
Curriculum Development	New Technology for Learning
Eastern European	Postgraduate Issues
Educational Development Research	Quantitative Studies
FE/HE	Student Development
Funding	Vocational Qualifications
Graduate Employment	

Benefits to Members

Individual

• The opportunity to participate in the Society's networks

- Reduced rates for the annual conferences
- Free copies of *Research into Higher Education Abstracts*
- Reduced rates for *Studies in Higher Education*
- Reduced rates for *Higher Education Quarterly*
- Free copy of *Register of Members' Research Interests* – includes valuable reference material on research being pursued by the Society's members
- Free copy of occasional in-house publications, e.g. *The Thirtieth Anniversary Seminars Presented by the Vice-Presidents*
- Free copies of *SRHE News* which informs members of the Society's activities and provides a calendar of events, with additional material provided in regular mailings
- A 35 per cent discount on all SRHE/Open University Press books
- Access to HESA statistics for student members
- The opportunity for you to apply for the annual research grants
- Inclusion of your research in the *Register of Members' Research Interests*

Corporate

- Reduced rates for the annual conferences
- The opportunity for members of the Institution to attend SRHE's network events at reduced rates
- Free copies of *Research into Higher Education Abstracts*
- Free copies of *Studies in Higher Education*
- Free copies of *Register of Members' Research Interests* – includes valuable reference material on research being pursued by the Society's members
- Free copy of occasional in-house publications
- Free copies of *SRHE News*
- A 35 per cent discount on all SRHE/Open University Press books
- Access to HESA statistics for research for students of the Institution
- The opportunity for members of the Institution to submit applications for the Society's research grants
- The opportunity to work with the Society and co-host conferences
- The opportunity to include in the *Register of Members' Research Interests* your Institution's research into aspects of higher education

Membership details: SRHE, 3 Devonshire Street, London
W1N 2BA, UK. Tel: 020 7637 2766. Fax: 020 7637 2781.
email: srhe@mailbox.ulcc.ac.uk
world wide web: http://www.srhe.ac.uk./srhe/
Catalogue: SRHE & Open University Press, Celtic Court,
22 Ballmoor, Buckingham MK18 1XW. Tel: 01280 823388.
Fax: 01280 823233. email: enquiries@openup.co.uk

Publications from IMHE

The OECD Programme on Institutional Management in Higher Education
Since 1969, IMHE has monitored developments in higher education during the periods
of growth, retrenchment and reassessment. IMHE assists higher education institutions,
through analysis and the sharing of information, experiences and expertise, in addressing the challenges of growing demand, increased autonomy and accountability, greater
competition and internationalisation. IMHE membership includes institutions, government agencies and nonprofits organisations dealing with issues at the interface of higher
education policy and management, from 30 countries in Europe and other parts of the
world.

Higher Education Management
The Journal of the OECD Programme on Institutional Management in Higher Education (IMHE). Higher Education Management addresses administrators and managers
of institutions of higher education and researchers in the field of institutional management. It covers the field of institutional management through articles and reports on
research projects, and provides a source of information on activities and events organ-
ised by OECD's IMHE.
OECD code 8900001P
ISSN 1013-851X **Language** English **Medium** Paperback **Periodicity** 3 times a year
Also available in French

The Response of Higher Education Institutions to Regional Needs
Report prepared by Paul Chatterton , under the guidance of John Goodard, from the University of
Newcastle upon Tyne
What contribution do universities make to the development of the regions they are
located in? How can the resources of universities be mobilised to contribute actively to
the development process? The challenge addressed in this book is how should higher
education institutions respond to demands which are emanating from a set of actors and
agencies concerned with regional development and thus help reach national objectives.
This book is based on case studies presented at various conferences focusing on Australia, the Baltic State and Scandinavia, continental Europe, the United States and the
United Kingdom. The case study material is supplemented by other sources of information about national higher education policy, including major national surveys of

higher education in Australia, Finland and the United Kingdom, each of which embraces the regional agenda.
OECD code 891999111P1
No. pages 152
Also available in French
ISBN 92-64-17143-6

Quality and Internationalisation in Higher Education
Edited by Hans de Wit, Universiteit van Amsterdam, the Netherlands, and Jane Knight, Ryerson Polytechnic University, Ontario, Canada
For many universities and other higher education providers, internationalisation is becoming an integral aspect of their teaching, research and public service roles. And increasingly institutions are operating in a global market in which quality assurance and assessment are particularly important and sensitive issues.

This book discusses some of the challenges of ensuring quality internationalisation, and provides a framework to assist institutions in designing and reviewing their own strategies and policies. Analysis of the evolving policy environment is contributed by internationally recognised experts. Case studies from Australia, Finland, Kenya, Mexico, Poland and the United States are included. The book also presents the Internationalisation Quality Review Process (IQRP): a unique practical tool for institutional leaders and managers who wish to develop the international dimension of their programmes and services
OECD code 891999101P1
No. pages 268
Also available in French
ISBN 92-64-17049-9

IMHE publications are available from: OECD - 2, rue André-Pascal - 75775 PARIS Cedex 16
Tel: 33 (0)1 45 24 81 81 - Fax: 33 (0)1 45 24 19 50
Internet: www.oecd.org/bookshop